Poem

~~~~~~~~~~~~~~~~~~~~~~~

Page

~~~~~~~~~~~~~~~~~~~~~~~

To

~~~~~~~~~~~~~~~~~~~~~~~

From

~~~~~~~~~~~~~~~~~~~~~~~

THE BLAZE AND THE *Balm*

Personal Life Experiences Poems & Reflections

Virginia Jack

Tate Publishing, LLC

"The Blaze and the Balm" by Virginia Jack

Copyright © 2004 by Virginia Jack. All rights reserved.

Published in the United States of America
by Tate Publishing, LLC
127 East Trade Center Terrace
Mustang, OK 73064
(888) 361-9473

Book design copyright © 2004 by Tate Publishing, LLC. All rights reserved.

No part of this publication may be reproduced, stored in a retrieval system or transmitted in any way by any means, electronic, mechanical, photocopy, recording or otherwise without the prior permission of the author except as provided by USA copyright law.

Scripture quotations marked "KJV" are taken from the Holy Bible, King James Version, Cambridge, 1769.

ISBN: 1-9331487-8-0

Dedication

This book is dedicated to the memory of my dearest mother, Ruth M. Hester-White. So much of my encouragement came from my mother while I was growing up and even when I was attending college, there in my hometown of Indiana. I can yet hear her saying, as I complained about how far I had to walk to grade school and later on high school, through the rain and snow,

"Don't' look at how far you have to go be thankful for how far you have gone."

One of the attributes that my mother displayed was humbleness and the other was humility. A sweet and kind woman with a gentle touch, Mother of seventeen children. She inhibited an air of elegance, a royal child of the King with keenly wisdom and knowledge. She was tall and graceful, and like a princess she actually flowed when she walked. She held her head up high. I will always remember her gentleness and godly spirit. She believed that I could excel in anything I set out to do.

She was a virtuous woman, Her price was far above rubies. **(Proverbs 31:10)**.

*I reverence her memory.
"Peace"*

Acknowledgements

I would like to thank my Lord and Savior Jesus Christ because, **"Every good gift and every perfect gift is from above" (James 1:17).** I would also like to acknowledge all of my sisters, brothers, and friends who encouraged me to go a step further after hearing my poems, to have them published. I have written out of my heart and soul, a hidden, continuous spring let loose, saturating, watering every dry place: mind, body, spirit, and being. A "Blaze of Fire" and the content was soothed, contained, and comforted only by the "Healing Balm" from above.

Everything and everybody that I have ever come to know has, in some way, whether positive or negative, given me input to share with you in this book. It may have been in the form of opinion, opposition or agreement, but it all has helped to influence the present outcome of my life and my heart's bank. I am thankful for all of the leadership from home, school, and the church that has in some positive way guided my steps. I acknowledge and am thankful for my present pastors, Billy Joe and Sharon Daugherty of Victory Christian Center, in Tulsa, Oklahoma, whose ministry has been valuable to me in encouragement with the Word of the Lord. Their international vision has helped me to see how great the need is in that field, both natural and spiritual and the part I must participate in.

I also acknowledge the pastor and his wife who presently shepherds my childhood church, Elder Joseph and Evangelist Norma Alford of Bethel Congregational Church of God in Christ, in Hammond, Indiana. There, at the age of about four years old, is where I first began to be tutored in the Word of the Lord. There I know that I am yet always loved and welcomed. The college that I have been attending, Oral Roberts University, has had a great impact upon and in my life. It, additionally, has helped to enrich my ability in expressing myself more fully, and to more efficiently carry God's Word and minister to His people. There are too many names to mention one by one of those who have influenced my path, but I would like to acknowledge and thank everyone.

Last of all, but not least, I would like to acknowledge my parents, who are deceased, Noah White senior, my stepfather, and Ruth M. Hester-White, my dearest mother. My childhood was a very busy one with many sisters and brothers; it ended with a total of seventeen of us. We were like the stones which were put into the chief priest's breastplate. My mother named her last child Jasper. She heard the name in the Spirit and never knew anyone with that name. When my brother Jasper was born I found his name in the Bible in **Exodus 28:15–21; Rev 21:11, 19.** Jasper was a precious stone and was the last stone to be set in the priest's breastplate on his garment. Growing up in a large family helped to strengthen me to be " . . . **Meet for the Master's use" (II Tim 2:21).** It is the good and the bad, the positive and the negative confrontations and experiences that flavors with peace the gifts that we later have to offer to the world. I have no regrets, no animosity, only love and thankfulness.

Virginia Jack

Contents

Foreword................12
Preface................14
Introduction................18

Poems & Reflections 23
Alphabetical Listing

Reflections (Only)................27
Alphabetical Listing

Poems & Reflections Categories:
Parts I—XII................29

Foreword

I have personally known Virginia Jack for almost a decade, and her joy of the Lord and over coming faith radiates in peace, love, and the power of God.

Virginia has been called by God to minister to the hurting women of all walks of life through inspiration, comfort, and encouragement. She has written this book of poems and reflections from her self experience, as well as from being a comfort to many other individuals.

Some of her poetry reflects the sadness and hurt one might feel when experiencing pain, loss, or disappointment, but all of it ends with words of encouragement, comfort and strength. I was experiencing a tough time of my life when I read the final draft of this book. Every poem and reflection brings peace to my heart and my soul enabling me each day to face an unknown tomorrow. I am sure everyone who reads this book will also feel the saturation of a victorious and worshipful atmosphere.

This book will help you to relax, to remove distress, and to know that the Lord knows everything you may have, or may be experiencing that is negative or positive. I would recommend this book to anyone who loves true poetry or may not be familiar with any of it at all. It promotes the attributes of encouragement, comfort, love, peace, as well as self esteem.

> Connie H. Keener
> President & CEO
> Alpha International, Inc.
> Cedar Rapids, Iowa

Preface

    I have always written poems and reflections but usually sporadically, and sometimes a year or two would pass with out my writing any at all. Most of the poems I did not even bother to keep up with not knowing they would be an encouragement to someone else. When I wrote at that time, I don't remember digging into the depth of what I will be sharing with you now. The poems and reflections that are now being resurrected are really a collection of true feelings, experiences, and outcomes over many of the years of my own life. I finally, again, sat down and began to write, after an unusual gravitating urge to do so. I found myself writing poem after poem along with reflections, even as many as ten during a two-to-three-hour sitting. I began to express some years of what seemed to be bottled up inside of me. I tell you, it was quite a relief to finally be able to say many of the things that I have been feeling and holding inside for these years.

    In some of what I have written, I speak of nature because it is one of the things I truly love and can relate to. The seasons, greenery, flowers, and even when things prepare to cease, there is beauty. Perhaps it is because so much of the beauty comes back again and again as lovely as ever. Scenery has a way of being about solitude, relief, and yes, even comfort. It was here before us you know. In **Genesis 3:8** the Bible even speaks of God out strolling through His Garden of Eden—just viewing what was going on and looking for the human creatures that He had created. Jesus himself often resorted to His special choice of gardens to be refurbished and renewed with His Father. If you think about it, poems and reflections are very much like a garden. They put a variety of color, expression, mood, and fragrance in the air.

Several of the poems that I have written are my favorites and "The Myrtle Tree" is one of those. You probably will not comprehend the true beauty that I try to express in my opinion of the myrtle tree if you have never seen one. My advice for you would be to find a picture of the myrtle tree for your own curiosity and visual knowledge. I am sure you would then agree with me concerning its serenity and loveliness. In several places of the Old Testament, it speaks of the myrtle tree. It is truly a tree that seems to be transplanted from heaven, an anointed seed. Next, the poem "The Magnolia Tree" surfaced when I watched it all covered with winter, ice and snow, here in Tulsa, Oklahoma. After the ice and snow melted off of the limbs and branches, it was as green as ever and had lost very few leaves. However, I later noticed that all during the late spring and early summer, this very tree shed its leaves generously and grew new ones, along with beautiful white flowers as wide as your hand.

Next, the "Flower and the Tree" is a poem that expresses appreciation for material things as well as nature. I was able to explain the value of each. First of all, flowers, you primarily look at and smell, cut and put them in vases. Secondly, trees are used to build the interior and even some exteriors of the houses we live in, and there are even wooden fences around some of the yards. I think you will agree that flowers and nice homes are both lovely and can make you very happy; both of them compliment each other. A beautiful home is wonderful, but it could never take the place of lovely flowers for me.

Next, the poem "White Diamonds"

is another favorite of mine and actually describes the way the sunlight hits the river at a certain time on some particular sunny days. The whole river then glitters like a diamond show case. I believe that you will also benefit from the poems about loss, joy, happiness, intimate worship, healing, tears, victory, and many more. I am sure you will also find solace while interacting with the reflections that I wrote, as well as each synopsis located at the beginning of each category of poems in this book.

Introduction

It would seem that I would begin the sharing of my story with you by writing an autobiography and those were my first intentions. However, when I picked up my pen, only poems began to surface out of my soul. As I mentioned before, so many poems came so swiftly that I could hardly write them down fast enough. I could write ten non-stop before taking a break. For years I had never been able to express how I felt and all of a sudden, now, it was like a great waterspout gushing out of a huge rock through an opening in a mountain. Who will want to read it? I really don't know. All I know is that it is certainly a tremendous relief for me to finally share what I once could not. So writing helps me with all of the expressions, which are sorted out prayerfully as I go along.

Whenever I write, I can always write what I want to because it's my story and my song. I write to myself and for myself first, and then it can be helpful to someone else who is introduced to it. As you read let me remind you that this is not research, such as seeking out remedies through numerous other books or statistical information. Rather, it is my very own qualitative, personal observations and experiences of my story, my song, and my feelings. Research, I am sure, would consider most of what I have written as a mini autobiography of my tests, triumphs, and trials. Writing, as it probably relates to many other writers, is a source of relief for me. It is a magnetic pulling coming about frequently or sporadically from the collected poems, prose, lyrics, and metaphors of actual life happenings.

Maybe you can relate to the happenings. If so, then you have experienced some of them or are in the midst of trying to untangle and understand how to deal with similar issues. You will never untangle life though, but if you can be patient and **Trust God**, He will untangle it for you. David said, **"I waited patiently for the Lord; and He inclined unto me, and heard my cry. He brought me up also out of an horrible pit, out of the miry clay, and set my feet upon a rock, and established my goings. And He hath put a new song in my mouth, even praise unto our God: many shall see it, and fear, and shall trust in the Lord (Ps. 40:1–3).**

Jeremiah also was let down into a dungeon filled with mire, but God heard him and caused him to be delivered **(Jeremiah 38th chapter).**

As well as loss, pain, tears, and waiting, I have shared with you feelings of victory, love, de stressing, being busy for God, healings, worshipping, and remembering God. I speak to you from my heart's field.

The poems about loss express only some of the feelings that I had when dealing with the losses. Therefore, I want everyone to know that God always came through for me. He will always come through for you too. Loss is a rude interruption and brings with it for most of us pain, sorrow, and uncertainties. Sometimes you may not know just what you will do or how you will make it. You not only grieve for yourself, you grieve for those around you who loved your loved one so much. It can also be very difficult to watch your children grieve. So how do you make it, and what do you do? It won't take me long to tell you the answer to that question.

Put everything into the hands of the Lord. Trust Him right through the pain, knowing He is able and will move it and will make it bearable. It may take awhile, but this is where trust and faith come in. As one of my poems says, you have to be willing to begin again—no matter how many times. Just trust God. God's love saturated the pain for me over time and lovingly embraced me. The comfort that I received from loved ones, friends, and yes, strangers, I can pass on to someone else now. Let me tell you how I am doing today—just wonderful! God has done everything He promised, but I trusted and gave Him the chance to do it. He always shows up; He always comes through. We are all entwined with everyday life and what it holds. Sharing and helping and encouraging one another are the best assets that we have besides having God our Father, who also purposely uses us to help and encourage one another. My pain has now been erased but not the beautiful thoughts of my loved ones.

    Maybe if you don't know the Lord, you will be willing to be born into His kingdom and walk in His presence every day. If you are hurting and in pain, or have been at sometime, give God the chance to change your situation. Let Him soothe and take away your pain in His good timing.

POEMS & REFLECTIONS
(ALPHABETICAL BY TITLE)

A Continual Feast 224-225
A Love Like This 153
A Victorious Happy Child 243
All of My Days are Good Days/
(Reflection) 184-185
Alone But Not Lonely 104
Broken 68-69
Can I get a Witness? 50-51
Catch It! 231
Changed 236-237
Cultivated Faith 192
D.N.A. 116-117
Feelings (Reflection) 170-171
Fire Place 120-121
Flying High 228-229
Forgive (Reflection) 162-163
Forgive Me 52
God, me and you 140-141
Good Night Little Pudding 54-55
Good Returns 144-145
Hadassah 239
HE (Reflection) 172-176
Heart of Flesh 71

The Way I See It *216-217*
Thee. *219*
Though Petals Fall
(Poem & Reflection) *132-133*
Time. *89*
To You (Reflection) *78-81*
Train Yourself *194-195*
Trust *106-107*
Unworthy (Reflection). *177-179*
Wait. *263-265*
Wait on the Lord *112-113*
Water to Water. *74-75*
What a Flower Says *130-131*
Where Can I Hide? *94-95*
White Diamonds *126-127*
Why Love?(Reflection) *58-60*
You Give Me Love *152*
Your Words *193*
You're Counted *98-99*
You're the Only One *198-199*

Reflections
(ONLY)
ALPHABETICAL

All of My Days are Good Days	184-185
Feelings	170-171
Forgive	162-163
HE	172-176
How Bad is Your Pain?	102-103
In Tulsa Now (Poem & Reflection)	136-137
More than Enough	164-165
Reflection of My Past And My Present	182-183
The Blaze	166-169
The Flesh	180-181
The Presence	268-269
Though Petals Fall (Poem & Reflection)	132-133
To You	78-81
Unworthy	177-179
Why Love?	58-60

POEMS AND REFLECTIONS

(CATEGORIES)

PART I: LOSS (SYNOPSIS)-35

Loss *44-45*
Lord Don't Hide *46-47*
Patience. *48-49*
Can I Get a Witness?. *50-51*
Forgive Me *52*
Make You or Break You?. *53*
Good Night Little Pudding *54-55*
Our Star *56-57*
Why Love?. *58-60*

PART II: TIME & TEARS (SYNOPSIS)-63

Broken. *68-69*
Heart of Flesh. *71*
Make Over. *72-73*
Water to Water. *74-75*
Let's Begin Again *76-77*
To You *78-81*

PART III: HEALING OF THE PAIN
(SYNOPSIS)-83

Time *89*
The Healer Came *90-91*
It's not About Me *92-93*
Where Can I Hide? *94-95*
How Many Times? *96-97*
You're Counted! *98-99*
I am Healed *100-101*
How Bad is Your Pain? *102-103*
Alone But Not Lonely *104*
Open Up *105*
Trust *106-107*

PART IV: WAITING (Synopsis)-109

Wait on the Lord *112-113*
Receive *114-115*
D.N.A. *116-117*
I Am Part of Everything *119*
Fire Place *120-121*

PART V: DE STRESS (SYNOPSIS)-123

White Diamonds *126-127*
The Flower & the Tree *128-129*
What a Flower Says *130-131*
Though Petals Fall(Poem & Reflect.) . *132-133*

The Myrtle Tree *135*
In Tulsa Now (Poem & Reflection) . . *136-137*
The Magnolia Tree *138*
The Returning *139*
God, me and you *140-141*
The Dark White Night *142-143*
Good Returns *144-145*

PART VI: KEEP LOVE IN YOUR LIFE (SYNOPSIS)-147

You Give Me Love *152*
A Love like This *153*
Loving *155*
I Have So Much Love *156-157*

PART VII: REFLECTIONS (SYNOPSIS)-159

Forgive *162-163*
More than Enough *164-165*
The Blaze *166-169*
Feelings *170-171*
He *172-176*
Unworthy *177-179*
The Flesh *180-181*
Reflection of My Past And My Present . *182-183*
All of My Days are Good Days *184-185*

could sometimes be difficult to share your feelings with others because you have to go through all of the steps of painful reminders. But whatever you do for the glory of God, He will cover and keep you. At the time I was going through experiences of multiple losses, if I could have done as David talked about in the **139th Psalm**, I surely would have flown away to the highest mountain or descended to the deepest part of the sea. Perhaps I would have hidden myself each time in the cleft of the rock until all of the calamities were past. Maybe I would have gone to sleep telling myself that it was only a dream and awakened to a new day with no problems in it. There's a saying that you can run, but you can't hide. If you cover your head, your feet will show, and if you cover your feet, your head will show.   Some people try to escape hurt, loss, and pain by indulging in drinking, drugs, and relationships. Others just cop out into a private world and leave the care of their emotions completely to people trained to deal with them.

     Yet there are also people who pray and ask God to remove their calamities. No matter what avenue a person chooses or falls privy to, a process of time and procedure is involved.

Some additional areas dealt with are guilt, hurt, disappointment, shame, anger, nonacceptance, blaming someone else, blaming yourself, feeling nothing at all, not blaming anyone else, not blaming yourself, not having any guilt, not feeling any hurt, and having a synthetic acceptance.

I experienced a great deal of loss within my own nuclear and extended family. I express some of the feelings that go along with those losses. Perhaps the particular poems that I have written concerning loss will help or encourage someone to get up and keep on going. Loss is something you can never really prepare for, but you can cope with it and restart your life.

You can look around and realize what you have left and yet be thankful. You can appreciate the people around you who show so much love and concern. Some of them will always be there for you. In time you may need to be there for them. We really learn to care and share by the things we experience and bear. **People who contribute the most to worthy causes are generally those who have had some personal tragedy, or direct involvement with those causes.**

Nothing in the natural could have really prepared me for all I was about to go through. I never wanted to deal with anything difficult or unpleasant especially, death. However, by the time I was 53, I had lost three husbands to cancer. Two died with lung cancer and one with bone marrow cancer. Twice, left with minor children to finish raising, I struggled through the preliminary steps to get back to a normal as possible everyday living routine. I believe that the hardest loss to regroup from was the first husband. He died with lung cancer at the age of 29 years old. Being a profuse smoker and working in an unfavorable atmosphere at work must have added to his fate. I was 24 years old and had four small children from the ages of two weeks old to five years old. I was absolutely devastated, because this just was not supposed to be happening to me—somebody else I could have understood, but not me. I had not been prepared for this in any way. Being left financially unstable added to the distress of being deserted.

Somehow with the help of a few friends and my belief in God, I tunneled through the rough places. Coming from a very large family and having the support of some of my siblings also helped me to regroup. I didn't know anything about the grieving process and really didn't know how to pray properly. Because of this, I must admit it actually took some years for me to completely adjust back to normal.

In spite of my incompetence in grieving and in prayer, I did have help from a spiritual mentor named Sister Ruby who did a lot of praying for me. She began coming to our church and was great spiritual support for me as well as helping me through some of the days, before and following my first husband's death. When you are young you don't worry about death until it starts happening close to home or at home

However, it is certainly good to have someone around who can pray for you and with you. Sister Ruby was middle-aged and single and prayed all of the time. I felt that she was very anointed, and I had great respect for her as most everyone else in the church did. Once when she came to church we talked briefly, and I heard her give me a scripture to read. It was II Timothy 2, the whole chapter. The next service night, I went up to her and told her that I had read the chapter. She looked at me real strange and said, "I didn't give a scripture to you to read; it must have been the Holy Spirit".

I never even knew her last name. We just called her Sister Ruby. She disappeared as mysteriously as she appeared. It was almost like an angel appeared for "such a time as this" for me and then disappeared. There are times I wonder where she is now, or if she is yet alive somewhere. I was never able to find her again.

Along the road I have traveled, I have cried many tears, felt much heartache and pain. I have had much grief and sorrow and many uncertainties. At one time I felt that I was the only one in the whole world to be afflicted with such outcomes.

I would read the book of Ruth and was able to relate to Naomi and would say to myself, "That's me." In the Bible, the story in the book of Ruth, who was a Moabite, also tells the story of the mother-in-law Naomi. Naomi went into a foreign country to escape starvation with her husband and two sons. There the sons each took a wife from among the Moabites. Unfortunately, the husband of Naomi died, and finally, each of her sons died also. This left Naomi all alone except for her two daughters-in-law.

Covered in grief and shame, Naomi went back to the land of Israel. She took with her one of the daughters-in-law but was empty of her husband and two sons of whom she loved so much. Besides feeling ashamed, surely she felt partly to blame for she said, **"Call me not Naomi, call me Mara: for the Almighty hath dealt very bitterly with me. I went out full, and [has not] the Lord hath brought me home again empty: why then call me Naomi, seeing the Lord hath testified against me and the Almighty hath afflicted me?" (Ruth 1:20, 21).** For she thought it was something she had done personally to offend God to cause such tragedy.

Repeated tragedies and unpleasant situations will cause you to think and to comb over what part you may have played in them happening. Surely it was something you could have done to stop the calamities. But and if so, what then? Naomi must have thought of many things she could have done to prevent the death of her husband and sons. The first thought I am sure was that she should have never left Israel

LORD, DON'T HIDE

I pray that you will stay where I can see you.
Through perilous storm and weather's thorn,
Don't hide from me.
For all I've sown and journey gone,
There's much at stake.
Let my faith arise amongst the tide,
Is the request I make.
Let daybreak come and darkness run,
While I wait.
Hear my call and answer all
For my sake.

Virginia Jack

For sure He came and called my name.
He said, "Quiet yourself
I never left.
I never hide but am disguised.
Open your eyes and see the skies.
All around you, as they hover and dangle,
Are your God-sent warrior angels.
Fear not and don't be dismayed.
To keep you safe and one day
For you to see my face,
My life was laid."

PATIENCE

Patience is true.
Patience is sweet.
Patience is pure.
Patience grows wheat.
Patience is strength.
Patience is strong.
Patience holds mercy
In its arms.

Virginia Jack

Patience takes love.
Patience is like a dove.
Patience is not a lyric.
Patience is a spirit.
Patience really doesn't take long.
Patience is in this poem.
Patience thinks of someone else.
You have to learn to forget yourself.

CAN I GET A WITNESS?

Talk to your neighbors; talk to your friends;
You never know if you will see them again,
Especially if their souls are not ready
To meet their Maker with sins even petty.

If you've warned them about being lost,
Warn them again and tell them the cost.
It's never too late as long as there's life.
Tell them you love them and they need
Christ.

Compel them and tell them and offer to lead
Them in a prayer to cover their needs.
If they refuse, you won't have to think,
When they slip away, Did I do my deeds?

Virginia Jack

I went back home and decided to visit
My neighbor so fine and so attentive.
I was to ask about our friend;
She said, "He's gone with the wind."

Sure, I had told him to get himself right.
He said, "I know, I'll do it tonight."
More than once, actually many times
I said, "Stop, change your mind."

He didn't go suddenly, so he had a chance.
I hope he was led safely in advance.
It's not all up to me.
The seed I had planted,
Did you set it free?

FORGIVE ME

He walked the alleys, mornings early on,
Picking up bottles and metal scrap, just after dawn.
I stopped him periodically, see,
And bid come to church immediately.

He said, "I will, but I need a suit."
I said, "Bring your son, too, he needs the fruit."
Promises, promises, many times,
I hope somehow his way did wind

Back to the Father, back in his sleep,
To his Creator nice and neat.
Saved within, humbled without,
If I knew for sure, I could shout.

I wish I had done more
So I could be sure
That he knew how to pray
And he knew how to say,
"Forgive me."

Virginia Jack

MAKE YOU OR BREAK YOU?

Will it make you or break you?
Will you give up and give in
Or just begin again?

Will you hate or will you wait?
Will you refuse to be comforted,
Or turn your heart inside out?

Will you let the Master heal it,
Instead of concealing it?
And let Him put you back together again?

I will let it make me, not break me.
I will never give up; I will never give in.
Lord, my heart, you can mend.

I will love and accept, Lord,
All of your help
And just begin again.

GOOD NIGHT, LITTLE PUDDIN'

Here but a little while,
Weary-worn puddin' child.
I guess it wasn't meant to be.
God, He routes our destiny.

But I trust His judgment is fair.
Sometimes an unexpected answer to prayer.
I believe that it is for the best
God has laid you neatly to rest.

Early, God has called you home.
He is there you are not alone.
Of all the many types of love,
God's is truth; it's from above.

Virginia Jack

*As the flowers grow and birds sing,
Let the praises of God ring.
For I know that He always gives
Some to rest eternally and some a while to live.*

*Rest Eternally
Good Night   Sarah Niyah
4-12-96—4-23-96*

*From Your Loving Grandmother
Virginia Jack 4-29-96*

OUR STAR

There was a star high in the sky.
It shone for everyone to see.
It never faltered never failed.
It shone so steady, calm, & serene.
Through many years of inclement weather,
Rain and storm and wind,
It shone right through the darkest night,
Through troubles, sorrows, and the gloom.
It hung there, though
Seconds turned to minutes, to hours, to days,
Weeks, months, and years.
Though it seems such a long, long time,
It was scarcely a vapor if compared.

Virginia Jack

It lit the sky; it lit the streets
And raced the ripples over the creek.
It led my siblings, offsprings and me.
It hung there sometimes all alone.
If you look for it now,
It's gone.
Each of us will now have to be
That star for someone else to see.
It's your turn.

Dedicated to our grandmother, Lottie Tilton,
1902-2002
Big Mama, 99 years

REFLECTION ~
WHY LOVE?

Why love, when it is taken away quickly, so tragically, so forcefully?

Shouldn't it complete the cycle intended, rather than premature dispense? Who chooses who to take and who to leave? Do all take numbers? It is obvious that some cycles last a life time and others succumb to the minute.

Is it fate? Did you start too late?

No, all things work together for good.

Each presence passes to where it should.

Premature, lifetime, it's all a flower's breath to God.

A day, a week, one hundred twenty years, all a nod.

Love recycles new; it really never runs out. Look up to the heavens; look out over the mountains and the hills. Look out over the fields; see the wheat swaying. It is really people you'll see. Let your heart heal, and don't let your compassion and passion all run out.

There has been no mistake; it's not luck. Don't pass the buck. Yes, let nature heal your wounds, along with people, scenery, sounds, and everything and everyone that God has put around.

For every loss another 100 people or more will come into your life. Those that care, share, give of themselves; give their time, their blessings, and their love.
Let all of this help to heal you. Do not conceal hurt, disappointments, and devastation; it will destroy you. Talk about it; pray about it; share yourself; help somebody else.
We all take numbers; it is called love. Our help comes from above through those here that embrace us. You see them; you see Him. "He sent from above, He took me, He drew me out of many waters" **(Ps. 18:16)**.

My back was ripped, burned, and sunned, what pain! My anguish poured through every vein. Then my eyes could no longer see the sunlight for where I stood; the clouds finally covered it up. Though my backed burned; my heart turned freezing cold. My feet refused to carry me; my cross seemed too heavy to hold.

Somehow, in love, I opened up my hands; I touched my Master's hem. My brokenness began to heal. I began to see what was real.

Instead of looking at what was taken, I began to add up all that I had left. If it were but one soul then that was worth more than the whole world.

Like a lost sheep, my Master found me and sent those around me to pour in the oil and wine into my wounds and hurts. Through love there is nothing impossible.

PART II
TIME & TEARS
(Author's Synopsis)

Time and tears are subjects that go together. Most unpleasant tears come about because there is not a known time, a reasonable distance between what we are facing and the end of it. We cannot see a definite time established to completely diminish whatever caused the tears in the first place. In other words, you can't count on tears and pain going away in two weeks or two months or completely away in one year. Since it is a process with many circumstances to take into consideration, different people will get over things within different time spans. Someone may grieve over losing a well-loved family pet; another, the loss of a sibling; and yet another may have to get over a tragic accident taking away a whole family.

You really cannot criticize because one person may grieve a little longer than another. Some people get busy and go on with life right away. This may help them to forget or to cope while others may grieve and much slower get over what is weighing their heart.

A good, healthy tear gathering can be good for the soul, but extended too long, it can weigh down the heart, spiritually, mentally, and physically. It was not meant for us to grieve and cry every day all of our lives. We can give things to God, and He will lift up our load and take it. Tears may help to lift the load a little, but God is the permanent lifter. I experienced crying and also not crying at all. Not crying at all can have an unhealthy effect. Even Jesus cried when Lazarus died. It says, **"Jesus wept" (John 11:35).** People cry for various reasons, and some do not cry no matter who dies or what happens. That is not to say they do not feel the effect from the problem or unhappy situation. It may just mean that they grieve in another way. It may be unhealthy though.

Many things can cause us to weep, but God has prepared a way out of our sorrow and disappointments. We can give it to Him. Tears are a way of being relieved of some of the stress that goes along with the disappointment, whatever it is. Some people pray and look to God to remove their heartaches and pain that are felt. Crying really does not prove that you love the person that everyone may be feeling anguished over. Some people grieve and cry because there is so much they should have done and said and didn't, and that opportunity is diminished with the person deceased. So some grief is because of neglect.

However, God is such a forgiving God until He forgives us for all of our sins, faults, mistakes, and disobediences. Therefore, we must learn to forgive ourselves, dry our eyes, move on in life, and find someone to bless.

We do know that, at times, God is moved by tears when they are sincere and especially when they are combined with either: prayer, fasting, denials, supplications, thanksgiving, or worship. God is very tenderhearted and provides a way for us out of all our temptation and distress.

He will also forgive us for all of our shortcomings. David did not mind praying and crying out to God whenever he felt the need. He said **"Because He hath inclined His ear unto me, therefore, will I call upon Him as long as I live" (Ps. 116:2).** When I finally realized that I could give everything to God, I didn't cry as much. I no longer felt so alone and deserted or that no one could feel or know what I was going through. If you do not know this you may spend quite a bit of your time just crying to no avail. You cry without talking to or involving God in your calamities. God is always waiting and listening for your voice, which is different from anyone else's. As every mother knows the cry of each of her children, God knows the sound of distress each person makes. Once one of my siblings was crying, and while I just knew the one it was and told my mother so, she said that wasn't the one. Of course we found she was right when we went to check. A mother generally knows the cry of her child.

God knows each one of us, and every cry or voice is different. He knows my voice from everyone else's in the world. I don't even have to tell him my name. Every hair on my head is counted, whether it is black or white **Matt 10:30: "But the very hairs of your head**

are all numbered." If the hairs on your head are numbered, then God also sees all of your tears and knows what they are for. They are precious. **Psalms 56:8 says, " . . . Put thou my tears into thy bottle: are they not in thy book?"** Therefore, our tears are presented and recorded in heaven. So rather it is tears of sorrow or tears of joy, none will go to waste. But everything takes time. With time all of your tears can be wiped away. They will be replaced with contentment and comfort.

BROKEN

Broken, oh so broken in heart,
Shattered dreams falling so far
From what was anticipated so clear,
Drifting further and further each year.
Pathway seems dim out on the limb,
Came to my end, hopeless within.

Lord, what is it you want? What do you need?
What are the requirements for you to seed
Into my life, my heart and soul?
To answer my prayers like I was told?
To encourage my way, brighten my day?
Lord, when will the waves be still?

My requirement is sure and it is small.
Humble yourself and be broken, that's all.
For if you are broken then I can mend and
Sew you back together with me within.
I'll guide your path; I'll be your light.
I'll be there with you day and night.

Virginia Jack

Don't dream, don't fret, the end is not yet.
You came to your end so I could begin.
You walked out of yourself and came into my glory.
The airways were open; I heard your story.
I needed a vessel clean and washed to seal,
Broken and yielded, patient and real.

I watched you fall and helped you up.
I stayed the billows when they got rough.
My eyes never left you; my love was calm.
For all heartbreak and hopelessness, I am the balm.
I saw all of your tears and all of your trouble.
For all that you anticipated, you will have double.

Virginia Jack

HEART OF FLESH

She was so strong,
Could bear alone,
Never cried
No matter who died,
But had lots of love
From up above.
She struggled through storms,
Didn't waver though torn,
Never complained,
Faith heaven aimed.
She fought lion and bear,
Faced the enemies stare,
Stood like a tower,
Cried, when receiving a lovely flower.

MAKEOVER

The clarinets blew and sent their melodies through.
The violins whined, Come with us and dine.
The saxophones paced and blended with grace.
The organ sent its wisdom into every prism.
The trumpets warned, Keep it simple and clear,
The message you want everyone to hear.
The drums blended and supported the gathering,
Gently giving their pecks of approval.
The guitars carefully picked out and
Sent each note to join the others in the band.
The trombone gave them a hand in the unison plan.

Once all blended, they thought they would send it
To someone in need of a makeover,
Where the woes of life were trying to take over.
Change your thinking; tune your ear.
Hear what the Spirit is saying, dear.
There is a message; it will tell you what to do.
To wipe away tears, change your apparel too.
You prayed for a change to be arranged.
It's here; accept it; you'll never be the same.

THE BLAZE AND THE BALM

WATER TO WATER

Water to water, creek to creek,
Lake to lake, river real deep,
Somewhere in the middle they meet,
But my tears they joined the sea.
For they all ran out of me
And sorrow silently crept,
And I will admit that I wept.

The tears they flowed to find a fold
But none was here that could hold.
Measured without and discerned an overflow,
Determined, no other place to go.
So all that came from me ran into the sea,
Along with snow, sleet, hail, and rain—
All comes from our God's domain.

I wonder if over the trillions of years
The seas and oceans are God's own tears
Collected for all of us to see,
And billows, waves, and tides to hear.
My tears, they flowed and added to
The mist, vapor, and all the dew.

Virginia Jack

They also were a relief from stress
To give my weary heart a rest
And heal my soul and call it blessed.
Tears, they were made to gush
For the overflow of things life push
Into our paths and crowding our thoughts,
Remembering battles already fought.

But when we mingle tears with prayer,
The Lord will always meet us there.
Thrown out on the water ways,
They will return in not many days,
Destroying all fear and doubt,
Bringing victory, putting all unbelief out.

Jesus wept for His enemies and friends
Through tears of blood from brow and side.
They flowed and found where I reside.
So now when my tears begin to flow
I always save some for souls.
I have also learned over the years
To surely bathe my prayers with tears,
Bringing fresh relief and blessings of peace.
I learned to pray every day
And to read my Bible the very same way.

LET'S BEGIN AGAIN

Let's begin again; I know you didn't win.
You dropped out before finishing your course.
You got very tired, your load too heavy to haul.
You were unaware you didn't have to carry it at all.

Next time, listen to your heart and not your head.
Don't let your emotions dictate your stead.
For every cross and every hill, victory is revealed.
The blood ran; water flowed; for all you owed, it is sealed.

We all have made mistakes at times and turned the wrong way,
Perhaps to better show us how to stay
Close to God in prayer, not choked out by pride or despair,
Running our race, keeping our pace, receiving grace.

God—He saw you fall wayward by the wall
And sent to help you up—an angel on call.
He watches your every move, but you're the one to choose

The good path to take or the opportunity to loose.

*You say, "I've gone too far to backtrack from this mire.
I have waited too late and took the ungodly bait.
I have dug too deep from this hole to creep
Back to my loving Master's heavenly feet."*

*Let's begin again, and I will tell you when.
The sooner will be a lot better for you.
Come back to your Savior's gentle touch.
You didn't know that He loved you so much.*

*The enemy tricked you with doubt and left you without.
He told you, "You'll never make it back in rags."
But one thing he failed to consider— the cross that Jesus dragged,
The shoe He threw over you, so you could wear His tag.
It says, "I am the righteousness of God"* **(II Cor. 5:21).**
"I am redeemed" **(Ps. 107:2).**

REFLECTION~
TO YOU

I don't know exactly what you've been going through or for how long. I don't know your past or when you were born. But I do know trouble has now or at sometimes worked its way into your day. Though some of you have knelt and prayed, others just don't know the way: The way to humble down or the way to look up; the way to deny yourself and drink from your Father's cup.

The thought of Time has a way of weakening those in line. Especially if they don't understand how it winds. Time is a part of God's Word because He established and spoke it into existence. And God said, **"Let there be..."** **(Gen. 1:3)** *and the very things appeared. Time will bring forth an answer, a solution and, if allowed to run its course, a revolution.*

The enemy fights against time and tries to drag it out, long and full of misery. Minute-by-minute madness, day-after-day sadness. Things were not meant to be that way. If properly left to do its work, time will work for you. It takes faith to allow time its time, too. Time can hold whatever is happening or has happened. Time has to answer to God. It winds back with full report. God asks, "Time, what have you done? Have you erased the pain, or did you leave things the same? Have you calmed the heart or did you leave it broken apart?

You cannot come back to me void, so what is your conclusion of the matter?"

Time answered, "Your most Holy Grace; I tremble near your face, and I dare not return with a void reply. I have accomplished that which would let me try, to heal the wounds, pains, troubles, afflictions, and heart losses. Only have I left undone and unfulfilled those whose consent would not give. They did not want to live but drown in their own tears, sorrow, and troubles' blight. When offered time repeatedly, they wanted to fight. They chose to keep what they felt comforted them the most: self pity, sorrow, and what they remembered and could boast. They wanted what they could feel and see, imaginations and what used to be. I told them if they would hold my mane, I would take them into godly change." Another dream, another pace, winners will triumph over another race when they begin to realize everything revolves around time.

The Blaze and the Balm

Time was at the cross when our Savior died, and time went on, for our Savior had to rise. In time, our Savior was returned to the right hand of His Father and with love's compelling, left nothing void. Time returned back to us with the Holy Ghost and a mighty burning fire. Time was with the children of Israel in the desert when needs were dire. Time was with Paul and Silas, and even Peter in jail. It was just a matter of time, and they were released by heavenly bail.

Daniel waited in time for an answer for his sent prayer, 21 days. The enemy fought to stop it, but the angel Michael made him drop it.

Time is always on his job, sent by the Word of God. You will never be able to rob time. It has seen many suns swell over the horizon and moons displayed in the secret of darkness. It has seen troubles come and people born and saw them go. God spoke in wisdom and told time to go below. God has never been in time; it's only yours and mine. So you wouldn't have to suffer forever, pain or distress. Time divides and subtracts and, to God reports back. Time also supervises nature and tells it when to rest, go to sleep, and wake up. Time tells all when to give birth, timely or untimely.

*Time moves on and never stands still unless God agrees for it to, like He did for Joshua in **Joshua 10:12-14**, when time, the sun and the moon stood still for a whole day. Whatever God has promised will surely come to pass. God spoke and Time heard. Allow yourself time but don't sit down in it because Time will go on its way. Time will not allow his report to God to be void or late.*

Let the sun shine and the warmth from its rays singe the ends of your broken and opened pain veins. In time, but not dragging behind, let your change revolve into wholeness of spirit and body. Forgive; forsake blame.

We must let go of all our disappointments, yours and mine.

PART III:
HEALING OF THE PAIN
(Author Synopsis)

Most people do not see pain as a sore or an injury that needs to be healed. But when you begin to understand the very impact that stress can have upon one's life and body, perhaps you can see pain the same way. Pain, in most cases, can be paralleled with sickness. In other words, it must be dealt with and treated, or it possibly could cause serious harm to your body mentally and physically. Pain is something none of us likes to feel or cope with. If only one small part of our body begins to hurt, it affects us all over. For example, an injury to a small finger can cause a person to stop all functions such as going to work, participating in recreation, or even sleeping properly. Pain can cause your attitude to change and stop you from communicating with family and friends if severe enough. So the fact remains that pain indeed needs to be dwelt with and healed.

Pain—I have had plenty of it. But then, haven't we all? There are different types of pain such as mental and physical. Can you remember the first time you felt hurt about something that involved pain, or you cried because you were hurting so bad? For some of us, that was many years ago—maybe just a young child. Maybe you wanted something your parents would not buy for you. Maybe you didn't make the basketball team or baseball team that you wanted to be on, or the cheerleading squad. It also could have been the loss of a pet or loved one or just plain old somewhere you wanted to go. There are big hurts and little hurts, but they have one thing in common—they all hurt. Some even enough to cry. People that are hurt and weak try to lean on someone strong at that time, or they pull away from everyone. Regardless of the type of pain it is, mental or physical, it must be dealt with.

While visiting in the hospitals, I noticed the way that the nurse checked the patients' pain levels. She would ask them, "How bad is your pain on a level of 1 to 10 with ten being the worst pain?" It is difficult to measure pain, especially when it is emotional. Sometimes you can measure it by how the person functions or how much he or she is willing to share with you.

Some pain is good pain they say, because it notifies you that something is going wrong in your body. People afflicted with leprosy do great damage sometimes to themselves because in some areas of their bodies they can't feel pain. Especially if the area affected is their hands or feet. If it is their hands and they pick up a hot skillet, they will not feel the pain from it and will get further injury.

On September 11 or 9/11 as they call it, when our country was attacked, we all had so much pain. Our whole nation suffered together. The good thing is that most of us bonded together and went through it, crying and praying and encouraging one another. What pain, unexplainable but bearable, with following the proper steps of sharing our feelings, as well as listening to how others felt. It certainly is better not to be alone because **Ecclesiastes 4:9, 10** even says that **"two are better than one;**

because they have a good reward for their labour. For if they fall, the one will lift up his fellow: but woe to him that is alone when he falleth; for he hath not another to help him up."

One of the problems I had when going through the pain of loss and disappointments was sharing it. Being kind of a private individual when it came to what I felt were my most intimate feelings, I suffered alone inside of me. Of course, I had family and church that ministered to me, but **I yet kept a lot to myself**. I must admit that eventually I at least learned to pray through my own situations. However, there is nothing like having someone to share your calamities with and talk openly. I do appreciate who and what I had that did help me in some other ways. There were times when King David found himself alone when trouble came, but he encouraged himself: **"And David was greatly distressed; for the people spake of stoning him, because the soul of all the people was grieved, every man for his sons and for his daughters: but David encouraged himself in the Lord his God" (I Sam. 30:6).** To share what it is that hurts us is part of our healing. We can tell God about it and also someone we respect. Time brings about a big change too. To be healed of pain, we have the need for our souls to be healed too. We can realize the comfort we need when we invite Jesus into our hearts. He will save and bring along healing, comfort, and everything else we need.

Virginia Jack

TIME

Time is of essence.
Time is a chain.
It will pull away the pain.
Time is a healer.
Time is a revealer.
Time is on your side.

So let the tears come if they must.
Let the groaning resurrect,
Your heart's fallen crest.

It's a good thing to say what you're feeling.
If you keep up, time will never run ahead of you,
But it will leave you if you want it to.

Empty out, trade your pain.
Into your heart let it rain—
The season of healing.

THE HEALER CAME

Under Attack of the enemy,
Swiftly, fiercely, no mercy,
Hateful, unrepentant, loveless,
Murderous, and looking for cover;
But The Healer Came.

Under Attack, not expected, angry, jealous,
Running his course seemingly forever,
Unfair, unattached, didn't care,
Rebellious, loathsome, lying, hiding.
But The Healer Came.

The mighty hand of God
With His lightening rod
Struck down to the ground
Every intent from the enemy's mound.
Yes, The Healer Came.

Virginia Jack

The Healer came today.
The enemy got his pay.
With the sword he was beheaded,
Just like I had read it
The Healer Came.

Battle Battle, Clang Clang!
The war was on; the bell rang.
But out of the clouds the anointing descended,
From within me the anointing ascended,
And The Healer Came and defended.

The Healer Came.

To Mary E. J.

The Blaze and the Balm

IT IS NOT ABOUT ME

I found that all of my heartaches and sufferings
Were not about me at all.
You see, I built up this wall
To protect what I yet sheltered in my sea.
Selfishly, I decreed, Oh Me! Oh Me!

But as our Savior reminded, as I suffered for you
So faithfully in every area of the flesh,
Surely you, too, must.
Painfully, sometimes in loss, ashes to ashes and dust to dust.
Finally, I realized, I should not benefit the best,
From my frequently given test.

The blessings of my gained love and strength must be given
To my neighbor, strangers, and friends—
Especially those who have no hope within.

Virginia Jack

The true glory of it was that they might not fall in sin,

*While continually gaining strength
From the sea that Christ put within me,
Of sharing, caring, and bearing.
You see, when Jesus died upon that tree,
It wasn't about Him; it was about you and me.*

*His suffering benefited us as it pulled us from sins thrust
And then, Jesus created the sea of forgetfulness
With His own blood, sweat, and tears.
We were forgiven, saved, and healed.
We drew from it sharing, caring, bearing, life, and love
Through salvation's righteous Dove.*

The Blaze and the Balm

WHERE CAN I HIDE?

Where can I hide from everything outside?
Where can I go to escape the arrows flow?
There is no hiding in a physical space,
But I found a refuge in my secret place.

Under His feathers, snuggled in His wings,
I am safe from the torrents of sequential rains.
Hidden in the Cleft of that Rock,
In the middle of God's hand and it is locked.

I am safe from the stares and the glares,
Safe from the tongue with the tares,
Safe from the wicked and their teeth,
I am Blood cover-wrapped in the four-cornered sheet.

Virginia Jack

Hear me; hear me, those in despair,
I am here to tell you that God is everywhere.
Don't look to the stars or to the sky.
Don't try to wait until the by and by.

Listen with your heart, bow your knees.
You'll hear the wrestling in the trees—
The Holy Spirit moving, anointing, soothing,
The power of God near, your troubles to care.

Where can I hide? Where can I go?
Into His arms over and over,
Under His feathers, snuggled in His wings,
I found a refuge, quite a lovely scene.

THE BLAZE AND THE BALM

HOW MANY TIMES?

How many times can my heart break?
How many times can it tear?
There's a promise that says it will only
Be what I can bear.

How many tears can my eyes shed?
Can these many waters be held?
I suppose if there is an overflow,
They can run into the well.

My tears are living waters,
For they will not return unto me void.
They'll flee to their skillful maker, and
There make their abode.

Return unto me tears
But not in the form you left.
Return unto me tears,
My precious seed and rest.
I wait for your return;
Bring to me your best.

Virginia Jack

Bring the blessings with you,
Of all God's promises that read,
They that goeth forth weeping,
They bear precious seed.
They shall return rejoicing
With many glorious sheaves.

So don't get up early
Just to sit up late and fret.
Sleep well and rise up early
Knowing there is no debt.
My heart cannot break
Too many times to repair.
My tears are bottled up and
Presented before God's chair.

Tears are words unspoken,
A great mystery in mighty voice.
They are silently collected and returned
With blessings of my choice.

YOU'RE COUNTED!

You think you're not important, but you are.
You think you're a leaf forgotten, fallen afar.
Just as every hair is accounted for on your head,
You can't hide in the midst, nor can anyone be in your stead.

You think you have no value but you do.
You think you're not missed and that's not true.
No one can take your place, so come and run your own race,
And you can one day see your Master face to face.
He will say, "Well done."

Or will the Master say, "Who hindered you from running?
Who stopped you from coming?
Why did you hide your talent in the ground?
Did you think it would not be found?"

Virginia Jack

Will your talent be dug up and given to another?
Will it pass on to a sister or a brother?
No, you are more than a conqueror over every lie.
Now, hold up your sword and hold it up high.

You were born for this hour, and you must soar,
Carrying God's Word from door to door.
Every heart that answers to that knock
Will receive from God part of that Rock.

So take no thought for fleshliness or life.
Bury yourself now in the worthy light.
Remember it's not by feeling or by sight.
Obeying God's call is the only thing right.
Obedience is better than sacrifice.

To Valerie S.

I AM HEALED

I am healed, and it is just as real
As the wind that blows and the sun that glows,
The seeds they sow, and the flowers that grow
The tides that rise and the clouds in the sky,
As the breath I breathe and the aroma from the sea,
The moon that shines and the roses and vines,
Little bones that grow, coming from a mother's soul.

*I am miraculously connected
and resurrected.
I am healed.
Healings stripes provided freedom.
It came attached to the salvation pack.
If you believe, you can receive.
Bring along a friend to be healed within.
It's a done deal.
"By His stripes you were healed!"*
(I Pet 2:24)
*It happens when you kneel,
Down at the cross line,
Prepared for this time.*

REFLECTION ~
HOW BAD IS YOUR PAIN?

Perhaps the pain of our Lord and Savior was emphasized, because it's something all of us must get acquainted with. If it is not personal pain and suffering of one's own body, then it entails loved ones, children, spouses, friends, neighbors, and strangers. The most compassionate people hurt whenever they see anyone else hurt. They intercede, pray, and/or help in any way they can.

Yes, the suffering on the cross is a connection to many things. God looked down and saw all of the pain being suffered here on earth. Since Jesus was tempted in every area the same as we are, it is actually logical that He would have to also suffer pain. There is physical pain, pain in childbearing, sickness, loss, rejection, abuse, neglect, and alienation from God, separation from loved ones, hunger, cold, heat, starvation, and many others.

How bad is your pain? Many of us would rate that question in different values on a scale of one to ten, with ten being the most severe pain. The pain of the cross for Jesus was more than a ten, because He carried pain for everyone in every category. Now, multiply that times every soul in the world.

The Blaze and the Balm

ALONE BUT NOT LONELY

Alone, are you alone?
Are you the only one at home?
Are your friends or family too busy?
Or are you set aside too long?

No, I am happy singing my song.

Have the days turned into weeks?
Have the weeks turned into years?
Is there a longing for someone to greet?
Are things getting too hard to bear?

No, I'm in a heavenly affair.

I wake with prayer and praise.
I kneel with my hands raised.
I read God's Word out loud,
And I enjoy His heaven-sent cloud.
No, I'm not alone; No, I'm not lonely.

I'm really in a crowd.

Virginia Jack

OPEN UP

There, beautiful rays pushing,
Let the sun shine in.
Open up your curtains.
Pull them all the way back and view
What God has sent to you:
New light, a new day.
Do not waste its essence.
You cannot replace its presence.
Acknowledge the Maker of it.
Humble yourself to that so-great-a
Witness of your daily estate.

TRUST

I have learned to trust, and it didn't happen overnight.
It didn't take a week or two, nor was a year or two in sight.
Everyday, in some way, I am challenged to believe
That regardless of my circumstance, my Savior will relieve.
His love won't fail, His Word won't fade
In doing so, He's doing no more than promises He made.
Though I walk upright and straight, or fall unexpected,
He'll be there to remove the snare and applaud when I'm consistent.

Virginia Jack

So I believe that I'll believe and take Him for His Word,
For of anyone who would sin their Son, no one have I heard.
I trust that God will always be where I need Him most.
I am so sure; I take no thought and of Him often boast.
I know that I shall never ever have to be ashamed.
I have trusted all these years in Him and called upon His name.
No matter when, day or night, He answers just the same.

PART IV:
WAITING

(Author Synopsis)

Whenever you think of waiting, patience comes into mind. Of course you don't have to be patient to wait, but if you are, it sure makes a big difference. If you can wait patiently, that can help to remove anxiety and stress from your wait. We live in a society where everybody is in a big hurry; they eat fast and rush to make a time deadline. The Bible talks about waiting for the early and the latter rain. David in **(Psalm 27:14)** says, **"Wait on the Lord and be of good courage, and He shall strengthen thine heart: wait, I say, on the Lord."** He also said, **"I had fainted, unless I had believed to see the goodness of the Lord in the land of the living" (Ps. 27:13)**. Some people faint because they are so impatient while they try to wait. But while David was waiting, he believed that God indeed would do what He had promised to do. **We do need to see God's goodness right down here and now while we are in the land of the living.** In heaven will be no problem. My advice to everyone who reads this book is to **never give up!**

Coming up in church in a small, local neighborhood, our pastor often told us stories, some similar to parables. One particular story was about a man digging for gold. He dug and dug, and finally, he just took his shovel and angrily stuck it into the ground and gave up. He walked away from his many days and hours of sweat, hard work and digging and searching for gold. Not many days after he had left, another gold digger came along looking to find gold, and he saw the shovel stuck in the ground. He picked it up and started to dig. After digging just a short while he struck a gold vein full of gold. If the first digger had just stayed and dug a little bit longer he would have been a very rich man. Our blessings, deliverance, and answers are often staggered along the way as we go. Not giving up is a must because God has never reneged on a promise. Though some fulfillments take longer they will come; they will happen. In **Habakkuk 2:2-3** it says, **"... Write the vision and make it plain. For the vision is yet for an appointed time, but at the end it shall speak, and not lie: though it tarry, wait for it; because it will surely come, it will not tarry."** This is the same for all of what God has promised you. Sometimes it may tarry, but it will happen for sure.

Last but not least, remember how our Savior waited—the agony, pain, and suffering He endured. The burden of the whole world of sin rested upon Him, and for a short while, Jesus' very own Father distanced Himself from Him. For Jesus said, **" ... MY GOD, MY GOD, WHY HAST THOU FORSAKEN ME?" (Matt. 27:46)**. Job said, **" ... All the days of my appointed time will I wait, till my change come" (Job 14:14)**. **Will you wait for your change?**

WAIT ON THE LORD

You wait in lines,
No matter how much time.
You wait at the tolls
And backed up roads.

You wait at gates
For consent to take place.
You park and walk
Or trot and talk.

At night you retreat
To rest and sleep.
You rise up to meet
Your contracts to keep.

You wait on the doctors.
You wait on your friends.
You wait for attorneys
To let you in.

So wait for complete healing of your pain.
Listen to God as He calls your name.
He will never leave you.
He loves you too.

Wait on the Lord
With shield and sword.
Believe His Word
That you have heard.

"Wait on the Lord:
Be of good courage,
And He will strengthen [your] heart:
Wait, I say, on the Lord."
(Ps 27:14)

RECEIVE

*I came to the waters to drink
And had an unexpected treat.
There was heavenly milk and honey
All fixed right there for me.*

*I wondered in His glory.
I doubted not His love.
All was full and free,
Prepared so perfectly.*

*I could not refuse
Though left to me to choose.
I thought, is all this mine?
Then He gave me bread and wine.*

*A lamb was sacrificed
And manna sent from above.
My Father came Himself and said
I brought to you my love.*

*I came down here myself.
Couldn't send nobody else.
The job was a delicacy
To make sure you were freed.*

Virginia Jack

Nothing can bind or hold you
Nor have power over you,
Though a season it may seem,
But I sent an ax and a beam.

The ax floated in the water
For it had a job to do.
It couldn't sink before time,
The job was about saving you,

So that you could come freely
To drink and eat and rest.
Manna, milk, honey, and wine,
I saved for you the best.

Lord, I receive your milk and honey.
Lord, I receive your manna and wine.
I receive the sacrifice you sent.
I receive all of Him as mine.

D.N.A.

I am victorious in Christ; I win.
I am blessed again and again.
Over and over continual doors,
Open up; open up, from flow to flow.
Give; give rivers, reach high and low.

The abundance of waters are pushing,
My countenance is refreshing.
My slightest desires brought forth
Reminders of prayers worth,
Being filled through God's word.

I am in God's Word; I can see His desire for me.
It's to love me, not hurt me,
To never leave me or forsake me.
I am in God's will; I flow with His blessings.
I am saturated in the output of love's caressing.

Virginia Jack

He's got me covered from head to feet.
It is evident to everyone I meet.
I am intoxicated in His Spirit; I sway in the mist,
Rolled in the roll, wrapped in the scroll,
*Grafted into His own **Divine Nature** and **Affection**, Anointed gold.*

I am in the image of my Father.
I look like Him, walk and talk like Him.
Every negative part of me is overridden,
And at His table I have been bidden
To eat of His delicacies and drink of His wine.
Everything that is His is now also mine.

Virginia Jack

I AM PART OF EVERYTHING

Oh, how I hunger
For what's far out yonder.
But I found it's really near;
I turned my gaze and found it here,
Down inside, safe, and free
It was right inside of me.
I found God and I'm not ashamed.
He cleaned my soul and called my name.
If you hunger for what's far out yonder,
Bend your ear and your knees.
Ask God for mercy, please.
He will answer if you can believe.

PART V:
"DE STRESS"

(Author Synopsis)

We all need the time to relieve stress that may have built up over an extended period. Many situations and needs can all cause stress in your life. Also, not having the necessities that you need can have the same adverse affect as other stressful situations. While people may rely on many different ways to relieve stress, some choose to read and enjoy the experiences of others that have been written and left on record. Autobiographies and poems are only a small segment of what actually exists for one's pleasure and relaxation.

There are many ways that I choose to "de-stress" as I call it. Writing is one of them. Also: reading, painting, crocheting, gardening, meditating, sight-seeing of nature, prayer, and other things. When I am writing, it seems I am unloading an eighteen-wheeler truck or even sometimes a locomotive train boxcar. Some people can use recreation and traveling for such relief. God always intended for us to express ourselves, communicating our feelings and thoughts. We can talk to Him and with each other, and that can certainly be an option to help us de-stress.

The four seasons are good for view and relaxation because they break the monotony. I was raised in Indiana, so every three months would bring about a change. That is what we need every now and then—a good change. For sure it is necessary to do something positive. By the way, I like sitting and watching the river as it ripples. Additionally, I have a little hummingbird that visits my flowers frequently all through the day when I'm at home to see it. Now, that is one lovely little sight, hovering in midair, not long as my finger, eating out of each flower. It often stops to look in my living room window at me for several seconds, and then it flies away. Maybe it has taken up people watching.

Speaking of people watching, there was a little squirrel in my back yard in Indiana, which was quite a nuisance, in my flowers, bothering things. I would shoo it away. One day I was feeling a little down and sat down on a little stool in the yard, with my head slightly lowered. The little squirrel had never come very close to me, but this day it came within about five feet of where I sat. It stood there for at least two minutes and then tilted its little head to the side as if to say, "What is wrong with you today? I have never seen you like this." It stood there for at least another five or six minutes. Somehow that cheered me up because it seemed like the little squirrel even cared about how I was feeling. It may be that God sent it over where I was sitting for just that very purpose. **He is " . . .The only wise God our Savior" and He has all "Glory and Majesty, Dominion and Power" (Jude 25).**

WHITE DIAMONDS

The river rippled on its way today,
Quick and steady hurrying by,
Not slowing down where it resided at,
While brilliant sparking rays sat upon its back.

Collected raindrops and leftover snow,
Tell me honestly, where do you go?
City to city, state to state, diligently on your way,
If I could follow, where could I ride?
You're covered with diamonds from the sky.

Arm in arm, river and sun,
Working wonders as you run,
Sharing glares, shimmering brightness,
Showing off a genuine whiteness.

Virginia Jack

Rich and lovely Arkansas Sea,
Keep performing just for me.
I am taking a picture to live inside.
If it were possible, I would ride your tide.

Flowing down and on your way,
The more you go, the more you stay.
There does not seem to be an end
To all your glory and glittering fins.

Tomorrow will be another day.
The sun may refuse to shine this way,
But the river will not be blest to rest—
No diamonds or shining,
But it will keep running no less.

THE FLOWER & THE TREE

There's a flower and here's a tree,
But they are both the same to me.
One is in a vase by my bed.
The other gives shelter over my head.

One is fragile but makes glad my heart;
The other is a fence around my yard.
One is here momentarily and then it yields;
The other one hundred years plus may give.

Virginia Jack

One is scented roses, lilies, and flowering grass;
The other pine, walnut, maple, and ash.
The one is in cut bunches on the dining table;
The other is sawed, hammered, and stapled.

They both provide what I need inside.
They delight my heart and my eyes,
Sends warmth to my every joint,
Gives me joy at every point.

The Blaze and the Balm

WHAT A FLOWER SAYS

A flower says "How are you today?
I thought about you while away.
I wondered if you missed me too.
By the way I really love you."

A flower says, "I am so sorry
That I didn't call, No not at all.
I thought you might be blue.
Want you to know I love you too."

A flower speaks
When words are cheap.
Its beauty embraces receiver's view
And says, "Look how much I love you."

I love you more than I can say.
Just turn your head; look my way.
When you don't have the power,
Just say it with a flower.

Virginia Jack

It will prick the heart
And hit the mark,
Sooth within,
The forgiveness bin.

It is heaven made
And does parade
In heart's field,
Connects to what's real,

When all fails, words and mail,
Open up nature's veil.
Release just like a dove,
Genuine-scented love.

It will reach where you can't see.
It will touch so tenderly.
It will melt away the blue,
Carefully presenting you.

The Blaze and the Balm

(POEM & REFLECTION)

THOUGH PETALS FALL

Though petals fall and fertilize earth's heart, they will help to reproduce the next batch, of scenic beauty, a quilter's patch. Carefully sewn and woven into designated space. Fashioned, modeled, and lying in wait.

Petals never go to waste. They float through the air saying, "I don't care I will land where I can. It will always be the right place."

Nothing ever goes to waste, a look or smell or even a taste. The birds and bees, they feast at ease, on the crown within where petals cleave. We look and smell and they taste and eat, for it is good. Everything has a purpose here. It just depends on the time of year. When petals fall, they answer their call. Though not

Virginia Jack

quite like a piece of wood; they toil and spin not and fall where they should.

Virginia Jack

THE MYRTLE TREE

Looking out of the back windows,
It is a very wet day.
Leaning toward me, the myrtle trees,
Heavy with rain drops as they sway.

Shades of pink, so prosperous and so rich,
Bowing down to His glory.
Uniform, one accord, performing art,
Synchronized beauty, nature's heart.

Collecting mist rays and nectar,
Preparing for days less favorable,
Generously taking so you can give,
Many years faithfully live.

Never saw such beauty.
Now that you have come my way,
I'll thirst for your Love,
I'll search for your display.

So unique at every stage,
Replica of heaven's trees,
Loaned to us, anointed seed
For us to see, to smell, to breathe.

The Blaze and the Balm

(POEM & REFLECTION)
IN TULSA NOW

The river reflects beautifully.
It opened up a part of me.
Thinking back and looking at how,
My life was and the way it is now.
Just sharing a little part of me so
We can put it together in a portfolio.

Nothing will last unless you write
Your thoughts, intentions, and heart's bites.
So capture your moments; harness your will.
Put it on paper, tapes, and reels.
Someone will find comfort in your mind's meal.
Leave it on record; leave it unsealed.

The same lovely river has been here for centuries,
But no one has seen it exactly as me.
No one can express how it makes me feel,
For out of my heart is out of my field.
Beauty is everywhere you go.

Virginia Jack

If you can't see any, it's right under your nose.

You can find beauty in everything.
Push out the negative; see the King and Queen.
Everything was here before we came:
Already made, already named.
So care for it; romance it;
Enjoy it; enhance it;
Write about it; remember it;
Love it; share it one-on-one;
Leave it for centuries to come.

THE MAGNOLIA TREE

In the winter it's pretty and green,
Even with snow and cold on the scene:
Blizzard or sleet on each limb and leaf,
Winter wonderlands coral reefs,
Loaded with obstacles that winter has found,
Branches full of leaves hang down to the ground.
When it's all over and the bugle sounds,
They rise back up and never turn brown.
If asked they would say, "I have a spring decree.
I will then release my leaves off of my tree."
They will soon come back multiplied
With multiple flower blossoms a hand wide.

Virginia Jack

THE RETURNING

*I walked among the leaves
Overhead up in the trees and
underneath my feet.
Wind blowing, leaves rustling
and crunching,
Between my steps a steady munching,
Always happy to see you come,
Sorry to see you go;
However, as long as the sun keeps rising and
setting,
The leaves will return with nature's petting.*

GOD, ME AND YOU

The trees, the leaves,
The bees fly to their hive;
The eagles dive in the sky.
The hummingbirds hover over the flowers.
The rain drains, into the earth.
The snowdrops quiver at the start of the river.
The birds sing and bring on spring.
The fish swim, at waters brim.
Monkeys hop from limb to limb.

The frogs croak; Lillie pods soak.
Storm comes; everything runs.
Sun beams; nature sings.
Lions roar; airplanes soar.
Elephants lumber through the jungle.
Giraffes neck, baboons pet,
Rivers meet; alligators creep.

Virginia Jack

Tide turns; forest burns.
Man and woman meet, love repeats.
Marry, tarry, recreate.
Lakes and streams, ponds, and things,
Creeks, they meet under, over ground, and seep.
Everything drinks, otters and minks.

Fields and flowers, castles and towers
House, land, and sand,
Children, boys, girls, the world,
The wheat, the tares, the deer, the bears
*The sky blue, **you**.*
People, plants, animals, the elements, and ants,
*Land, stones, mountains, the seas, oceans, and **me**.*

THE DARK WHITE NIGHT

The dark white night was quite a beautiful sight.
The sky faded into darkness, and the ground was white.
Away in the distance there were some minimal lights.
They circled around about and were about two miles away,
And they beckoned, Come join us; you don't have to stay.

However, the weather was much too cold.
I could see well enough from my fold.
Dark white night, do your job and I'll do mine,
That way neither will come to any harm.
You complement the cold, and I'll complement the warm.

Virginia Jack

*Dark white night with the minimal lights
I can see you just as well with the snow all around.
You'll be more welcomed when it is found
That the snow has disappeared into the night,
And everybody everywhere will need your minimal lights.*

*The dark white night will soon be gone away.
It comes for a visit never to stay.
Enjoy it while you see it because it's a treat.
It will be some time before again you'll meet,
So relax and reminisce in your seat.
It's one of those things you just can't keep.*

THE BLAZE AND THE BALM

GOOD RETURNS

I sat and watched the snowflakes fall.
They gathered together like at a great dancing ball.
They heaped up in piles until it looked like bedding.
There was a spellbound loveliness that resembled a wedding.

Where did they come from? How long will they fall?
Who was the sender of them all?
The sender was God from up above.
He just wanted to remind us of His love.

He sends them down and then turns them around,
Back into the heavens they are bound,
But not before they fall into the ground.
It is a continual cycle, down up down, around and around.

He painted the snowflakes to remind us of Him.

Virginia Jack

Each one is different from rim to brim.
Each has its own shape and has its own size.
When He calls, they all begin to rise.

Each has a name; they respond to God's call.
They go where they're sent and accomplish all.
They feed the sleeping trees, vegetation, and flowers.
That will last until God sends His showers.

God loves and respects everything He made,
Even every little snowdrop and every little vapor.
They complete their journey and return for favor.
Obedient reward will be given to them all
When they are allowed to return again later.

Snowflakes fall in every life
To clean out sin and clean out strife.
They will fall long to complete their cycle,
Sent by the Word, earned from revival.

PART V1:
KEEP LOVE IN YOUR LIFE

(Author Synopsis)

Keeping love in your life is more than a verbal or physical gesture. It's having genuine love for your fellow-person. This also includes your close family members and mates. I say this because at times your most difficult love problems may be loving those who are the closest to you, or you hurt because you do love them, and they do not return your love in the same way. Sometimes you think you know a person so well only to find out you do not know them at all. This, of course, does not exempt you from having to love them.

It is times like these that we must bypass what we actually feel, and we must rely on how the Bible tells us that we must react. Then we have to pray and keep reading the Bible until we feel what we should. The Bible tells us that we must love regardless of others' responses. Jesus loved so until He was on the cross interceding for those who had crucified, beaten, mutilated His flesh, and nailed Him there on the cross. Jesus kept love in His life. A person can crucify you without physically touching you or even saying one word to you. It is often the silence that can be torturous, making your heart bleed so.

Therefore, keeping love in your life consists of the godly love we must have for everyone. Keeping love in your life is not to let it escape in the first place. It is much easier to keep love in your life than to try to replace it if it is gone. Being able to forgive is one of the prime tokens toward loving always. We must also, as Jesus, forgive people for the wrong things they are doing to us even while they are doing it. How can we do this? By elevating our minds above the obvious and concentrating on the reality of Jesus Christ in our lives. By acknowledging His love for us and patterning our lives after Him.

Once, I went to a football game to watch my son play. It just so happened to be raining very hard that day. The faithful fans, friends, and families had come to watch the team play. It was not only raining really hard, but as I remember, it was rather cold outside also. Even with nature seemingly against what was trying to transpire, there was electricity in the air. The cheerleaders had on their short, colorful skirts and tops, smiling and encouraging the crowd. They were chanting, "Elevate your mind; elevate your mind." They said this over and over. I will always remember that day because of that particular encouragement.

That very slogan has encouraged me through many situations. I remind myself to elevate my mind. I decided surely I could press my way through the situation I was facing. Especially if the cheerleaders could stand and cheer in all of that rain and cold, smiling, and the boys on the field could play with all of their heart, wading in a soggy, muddy, cold, and wet field. The cheerleaders had great love for what they were doing as did the players. Love takes effort and persistence and consistency. It also takes perseverance and sacrifice, sometimes spiritual—mental and physical.

While walking around a 5K trail located inside of the city park where I live, I always enjoyed looking at the scenery. It was quite pleasant, since various areas of the park had very different views to take in. Headed toward a large pond, the particular day when I was walking was a family of ducks. The colors of their feathers helped me to distinguish that the mother was in the front leading the way. She was hurrying along trying to quickly make it to the pond, and following her were about 4 or 5 baby ducklings with their father close behind them in the rear. They all waddled along in a straight line; while up in the air I noticed hovering about was a very large, black crow looking for an opportunity to attack.

From his actions, I could tell that the father of the ducklings was aware of this and was prepared to prevent the attack if it happened. He kept a watchful eye on the crow while the mother hurried as fast as she could toward the pond. The pond was a safe haven for them, giving them a better advantage in the water over their predator. Of course, I stopped to watch the outcome. The crow knew he was in for a battle if he were to swoop down and try to take one of the baby ducklings that day.

The ducks did make it to the pond alright, but I guess what I realized was the most important thing was the love the parent ducks had for their little ones. The love was unconditional, unto death if necessary.

  To me this was an expression of unselfish love. I guess this is the way Jesus felt about us when He was on the cross. He was protecting us from harm and from being destroyed. The old crow was like the devil hovering over to pick us off one by one. Because of the Love that Christ Jesus has for us, we do not have to be picked off and destroyed. It is left up to us to choose Jesus, and he will watch over us day and night. Keeping Jesus Christ in our life is keeping love in our life. We must have the same love for others and display it at every opportunity.

The Blaze and the Balm

YOU GIVE ME LOVE

*When all else fails and my way is hard,
When life rebels in my own backyard,
When my steps seem unsteady,
When I never seem ready,
You give me love.*

*When I am so undeserving
And things are so disturbing,
When trouble is falling
And discouragement is calling,
You give me love.*

*When the road seems to end
And nothing will begin,
When happiness tries to flee,
Being nailed to a tree,
You give me love.*

*You give me love.
You give me enough
Poured out of your cup.*

*You give me love.
You give me love.*

Virginia Jack

A LOVE LIKE THIS

Where will you find a love like this?
Can you purchase it in a kit?
Can you find it just roaming around?
Or can you catch it racing through sound?

A love like this has never been seen,
Because from heaven it was gleaned.
And all over the earth plentifully sowed,
Carefully planted and Holy Ghost strode.

So much love, enough for everyone,
Give neighbors, friends,
And your enemies some.
Not like any other love.
Only the Son,
Could give so much love one-on-one.

A love like this cannot be found.
It was freely given
From heaven down.
Receive it; you'll need it.
It was for test of time.
It endured the test
And on a hill did shine.

Virginia Jack

LOVING

Why are you so happy?
Why are you so glad?
Who has faded all you doubts
And cast away your fears?
Why are you so radiant?
Who drew the glow upon your cheeks?
Who brought the peace into your heart
And calmed life's blissful bow?
Why are you so loving?
Who whispered freedom in your ear?
Who cast your mountains seaward
And who washed away the mire?
Why are you so trusting?
Why are you so strong?
Who gave to you a two-edged sword
To keep away all wrong?
Why are you so sure?
Why are you so free?
Because I am loving God, and He is loving me!

I HAVE SO MUCH LOVE

I have so much love I want to give it,
So much compassion others need to feel it,
A burning desire that builds higher and higher,
To embrace life's cast away and silent.

I have so much love I want to shout it
To the tides, the seas, and the land about it.
A tempest filled, ready to spill
Over the brim, a sweeping giving.

I have so much love that I can only worship
And weep with praise to the Ancient of Days,
Crying be Holy, Holy, Holy, Holy in all of my ways,
Blessings, Blessings, Blessings, forever foundation laid.

I have so much love; it is a continuing flow.
I have so much love; it needs somewhere to go.

Virginia Jack

I am so full inside; there are wells and wells.
I am telling you now; I feel compelled;
I have so much love.

I have so much love; its turning and burning.
It has ignited my soul and made my life whole.
I have so much love; it cannot be contained.
It turns and swirls and dispenses like rain.

With all of this love, what can be gained?
It will draw to the cross the forsaken and lame,
The poor, the lost, the forgotten, and distraught.
Love respects all nations and will leave none naught.

God has given me so much love.

PART VII:
REFLECTIONS
(Author Synopsis)

Reflections are just that, saying how you feel about what has happened in your day, in your life or at any time or place. It can be about any thing or any subject. The reflections that I have shared with you have come from within me, describing how I have felt about certain things or issues. It also may reflect some revelatory inspiration that I heard in the Spirit. The reflections will say to you the things that I feel and believe, either because of experiences or because it is what the Word of the Lord has to say.

These reflections will impart unto you the intimacy of feelings when things seem to be going haywire. They will take you on a journey over many years though you can read them in much less time. They will imprint for you a visual portfolio of thoughts and actions. Though you will not have to bear the mental or even physical pain it may have caused me, you will benefit from what God did about the situation. Perhaps at this moment you are having your own time of uncertainties and disappointments. I pray that the positive end of all of my calamities (God) will take you by the hand as Jesus did Peter and cause you to walk on the water **(Matt 14:29-31).**

Maybe you can take note and create your own portfolio of blessings for every deliverance and answer that God sends to you. Later you can share it with someone else. We have the Bible here with us today because someone dared to write about the wonderful things that were happening to others and to them. Sometimes God just spoke to them and said, "Write." We received the Ten Commandments this way, along with the rest of our biblical scripture. Whatever you write and reflect of your experiences may be around for a long, long time should God delay Jesus' coming.

Throughout this book may your heart understand my momentary afflictions and realize that yours will not last forever either; mine didn't. Realize that God is faithful to those who love Him. Though many of us have the same experiences, every one of us would explain it, see it, or feel it in a different way. When you go through your dry places and come to your water spring, you will be able to write with confidence, love, and example. Even if you just write for yourself, it will help you to remember exactly what questions or misunderstandings you've had and, later, the revealed answer. Remember, what you write may be a special blessing for someone else.

FORGIVE

Lord, we have learned to forgive, and the best example of forgiveness is yours for us. Who else would have loved us enough to die? Who else would have agreed to suffer the pain—physical, emotional, and spiritual—that you did? Those closest to you fled at the very thought of what crucifixion or even being imprisoned entailed. They wanted no parts of the pain and suffering at that time. They did what none of them thought they would ever do. They fled. But Jesus, you being so forgiving, forgave all of them. Oh, how we also, will have to learn to love and to forgive.

Whenever I am tempted not to forgive or hold a grudge or an offense, I just begin to think of all of the things that the Lord has so faithfully forgiven me for. Even after becoming born again, repentance has been necessary in my life. It is so easy to speak too quick or think wrong thoughts about someone. There are things I have thought and it turned out that I was wrong. That caused me to take a good look at myself for I realize I had flaws that had to be removed.

Unless God tells you something particular concerning a person, it's best to just pray for them. Whatever He shows or tells you about a person, it is so that you can pray for them, not gossip or tell everyone. This will help you to keep a forgiving heart, when you take everything to God in prayer, even if you are mistreated. Just as God forgives us, He expects us to do the same with others. After instructing us how to say the proper prayer, Jesus said, "For if ye forgive men their trespasses, your heavenly Father will also forgive you. But if ye forgive not men their trespasses, neither will your Father forgive your trespasses
(Matt. 6:14-15).

REFLECTION ~
MORE THAN ENOUGH

Every cloud is unique. There are no two clouds alike. The sun never shines the same way twice and each day is different and unique. It never rains the same way twice; each time is different. The snow never falls in the same identical pattern. The wind never blows exactly the same.

God loves me in so many different ways, for He has a variety of love. He loves to love. His love for me is unique, and He knows exactly where I am at and what I need for each situation. God has an unselfish intimate love; it just overwhelms you. His love is contagious; so be in love with Him. Don't ever get enough of Him. As you keep seeking Him, your relationship will get stronger and more powerful. God's love will cause you to love others with no room for evil or hate. There also will be no room for sickness or disease; they will dissolve and will not be able to live in you. His forgiveness is like His love, it is forever.

So let the rain rain, the snow snow, the sun shine, and the winds blow. Let the clouds take their place in the sky. Let God's love continually flow, for there is more than enough. Because there is more than enough, it multiplies as it rises in your heart and mine.

Everything God does is unique, and it cannot be duplicated.

REFLECTION~
THE BLAZE

And the Blaze leaped up and reached for the sky up through the chimney but not without sound, color, and radiated warmth. It soothed my mind. The warmth penetrated all of the layers of my skin; it warmed my bones to the marrow. Each color in the flame caused special warmth to sink into my body and into my mind to different degrees. The warmth filtered out all of the fogginess of leftover tiredness and uncertainties from my mind and body also. The darker reddish orange in the fire seemed to sink in the deepest, stilling every unnecessary thought, relaxing every muscle and cell. My body cooperated, willing to hold captive those unusual moments and feelings.

The smoke from it all going up the chimney was a steady reminder that something was taking place indeed. And the sound spoke, "I am doing this for you, and it was ordained from the maker of heaven and earth *that I should provide this warmth and this array for you today. I have been used for many purposes, for once I was even responsible to light the night for the Israelite's (**Ex. 13:21, 22**). I consumed the sacrifice prepared by Elijah to prove that God is the only God and beside Him there is no other god (**1 Kin. 18:38**). I performed for Elijah when He was unsure of what to do and was running for his life from Jezebel. He came up into the mountains and I was up there with God (**1 Kin. 19:12**). I was in the burning bush that Moses saw as he kept the sheep in Midian (**Ex. 3:2**). Moses used me in a display of the power of God when persuading Pharaoh to let the children of Israel leave Egypt (**Ex. 9:23, 24**). I was the fire that consumed the guards of Nebuchadnezzar when they threw the three Hebrew boys into my pleasure. I could not harm the three Hebrew boys because they could not be burned, God was there with them (**Dan. 3:22-27**). Isaiah said, "…when thou walkest through the fire thou shalt not be burned; neither shall the flame kindle upon thee (**Is. 43:1, 2**).*

*I was the fire that was sent from God to destroy Sodom and Gomorrah for their many sins including homosexuality. I was so powerful until I destroyed the cities, plains, and all of the inhabitants of the cities, and everything that grew upon the ground. **(Gen. 19:24, 25)**. I was the fire that swept the chariot up into the heavens, which Elijah was pulled into **(2 Kin. 2:11)**. I am the fire of the power of the Holy Ghost in **(Acts 1:8)**. I sat upon the heads of those blessed to receive me on the day of Pentecost **(Acts 2: 3, 4)**. I am the fire that now lives in every holy individual that qualifies. I am the fire that Jeremiah spoke about **"But His Word was in mine heart as a burning fire shut up in my bones" (Jer. 20:9)**. I am the live coal taken by the seraphim, off of the altar, made by fire, which sanctified and anointed the tongue of Isaiah **(Isa. 6:6, 7)**.*

*Fire reminds me of God and of great measure, **"For our God is a Consuming Fire" (Heb. 12:29)**.*

*It also reminds me of hell because hell is about fire burning forever and ever, among other most dreaded things. No one likes to hear abut hell, or the lake of fire, but nevertheless, it does exist you know **(Rev. 20:10)**. It is a gamble to ignore hell and just hope you're okay and that perhaps you will hopefully make it to heaven. It's best to be sure, "be very very sure," as in the song <u>In Times Like These</u>, "that your anchor holds and grips that solid rock." So repent often, love, and live holy. Let the fire of God blaze in your hearts and let it be warmth to those around you even to their marrow. Let it burn the sin and sickness all out of your life by the power of God. Yes, fire is used for many things. The best thing is the fire of the Holy Ghost, which comes to live on the inside of us **(Acts 2:4)**. The worst thing is the fire in Hell **(Rev. 14:10)**.*

REFLECTION~
FEELINGS

God is very expressive. He will make known His feelings. If something hurts Him because of how He is treated, He will let us know. Following His communication with the prophets in the Old Testament, we can see clearly how God interacted with them. The prophets were used as spokesmen for God. God is very sentimental, and He is a Lover. He became grieved at times because of the sin in the lives of the people in the Bible. He became angry when they refused to stop doing wrong and used illustrations to show them how He felt. God destroyed many of them because of this. He was always quite thorough in explaining Himself and what He wanted done.

A very particular person, God demanded that everything be done, built, and performed in an exact manner. Noah was given specifications as to the size and shape and a complete description of the ark he was to build. Moses was given specifics to follow in making the portable tabernacle. This included the gold, silver, metals, precious stones and gems, color, embroidery, carving of flowers, and making of precious gold and silver pieces for that temple, among other things.

God has a specific way that He expects us to worship preferably " . . .In Spirit and in truth" living holy, and loving one another. When we follow God's plan of salvation it benefits us, not only spiritually, but physically, mentally, and naturally. We can do whatever we want to do, but there are recommendations for eating, sleeping, loving, and forgiving. They are all things which will help us to have healthy bodies, souls, minds, and spirits.

REFLECTION ~

HE

And He came down and brought to us a new element of forgiveness, a never heard of element of love, a new desire and focus.

Instead of a group-think worshiping concept, individual worship was established—one-on-one worship with God Himself. Not discarding group worship by no means but adding power to the corporate worship through individual autonomy. Each individual was now responsible for worship on a daily basis even before coming together with the group.

An intimate worship, one that happens to you on the inside—Passionate desire, an incubated relationship, one capable of growing and reproducing; The Holy Spirit, conceived on the inside of man/woman alike; An impregnation, resulting in a continual well of praise, worship, and thanksgiving; a twenty-four-seven guardianship for each individual alike—it was the Holy Spirit.

Never thought of, never known, the once infrequent visitor who came only periodically, the cloud by day, the fire by night, the lone star in the sky—the Holy Spirit, which came upon man/woman and faithfully left or ascended, could now be carried by the human body.

A continual feast, one sent from heaven by God and His Son Jesus, a direct connection to eternal glory now on earth, but it needed somewhere to live in order to be nourished and fed, to be exercised and fed by God Himself through His own Word.

A piece of the rock, the anointing only realized through salvation as a prerequisite—without salvation there is no carrying of the Holy Spirit.

A prepared vessel, garnished and swept that says, "Here am I Lord. Come in unto me for I have hired you. Let me worship and praise you. All has been paid for by my Lord and Savior Jesus Christ, He is my dowry."

*Salvation—paid for with blood, bruises, and great sufferings. His head became a river to hold the tears of many waters, as in (**Jer. 9:1**). Tears ran out of His side because his eyes could not hold them all. The pierce in the side, not in His heart but underneath, released the seeds. The seeds joined the blood already present, a humble conception, and then a humble birthing began with much labor. And yes, remember His own birth, in the humility of the stable; but ours began outside, in the open, not in the convenience and warmth of a partially clad stable.*

Jesus went from life, unto death, and then was resurrected back to life forever. So our Savior went into the womb of the earth, and the birthing was finalized in the resurrection of Him by Our Heavenly Father God.

A tabernacle within, a sacrifice permanently made for each of us, and the incense of personal worship could now take place inside of us. Holiness in a holy temple is the requirement for sustaining and keeping the Holy Spirit, which was afforded us through the suffering Jesus endured for our salvation and healing.

*A new forgiveness, a new love took place, even unto death. Solomon once said, " . . . **For Love is strong as death" (Song 8:6).** We now must say that love is stronger than death because our Savior loved us so that He died for us. He was then resurrected from the dead, taking power over death and hell. **"I am [He] that liveth, and was dead; and behold I am alive forevermore, Amen; and have the keys of hell and of death" (Rev. 1:18).** Jesus did this all because of love.*

The mystery of His love is this: **"For scarcely for a righteous man will one die: Yet peradventure for a good man some would even dare to die. But God commendeth His love toward us, in that, while we were** *yet sinners, Christ died for us" (Rom. 5:7, 8). Before you or I were ever born, Christ prepared for us redemption. Just like God prepared the earth for our physical arrival, Jesus prepared for our spiritual arrival. It is completed and sealed. Now we don't have to be in fear of eternally damnation, because Jesus died to free us and give to us the Holy Ghost down here that we might have power over the enemy, and have eternal life with the Father and the Son and the Holy Ghost.*

However, one thing is asked of us: **"And this is His commandment, that we should believe on the name of His Son Jesus Christ, and love one another, as He gave us commandment" (I John 3:23).** *Also,* **"We know that we have passed from death unto life, because we love the brethren. He that loveth not his brother abideth in death"**
    (I John 3:14).

REFLECTION ~
UNWORTHY

When I feel the most unworthy, is when I often feel the most anointed, and Lord God, You really do perform. Perhaps, Lord, it is your way of saying, as You have at other times, "It is not you anyway who moves, it is me." How lowly it feels, but perhaps that is an opportunity to experience You, totally at work without help from me.

My experiences with You have shifted over the last few years; maybe because I finally allowed You to surface all of my fleshly being. Maybe because I see even more so now, how helpless I am without You. You know as a young girl, when playing baseball at school, I wanted to cover all of the bases. No one else could be as efficient as I was, so I thought. When does a person finally get to the place that they feel in the center of your perfect will? With You running everything? Lord, You have often reminded me saying, "I Don't Need No Help."

One thing I have resolved to do and that is to never give up! I will please You and do things your way. Thank You for your patience. Without You, Lord, in my life, I would truly be hopeless. But with You I have found mercy, of which I am not worthy. The best thing I can think to say to You Lord is, "Let me remember to have the same mercy for those I encounter, as You have always had for me."

I am at a most humble dispensation in my life. Although I do not look back with resentment or anger, I cannot completely ignore all of my life's offerings. Even if it is just to see the part You have played in my being who I am, what I am, and where I am today.

Though I speak, not from a sinfully weakened state, but I do speak from a constantly humbling tier in your hierarchy. I humbly summit this reminder to You; to remember my state and also my desire to please You. Deal with me as You always have, according to my heart and not my flesh. I trust in your Word and know that your promises are true. I await your next decision and Word concerning me.

I know if I should doubt anything it should be to doubt my doubts, if there be any such thing in me. Lord, let my days be fruitful in every area of my life. I am dedicated to You and Your Will is my attire.

Signed, Virginia

REFLECTION~
THE FLESH

We have to live the most we can in the spirit as possible and live the least we can in the flesh as possible. Do not let your flesh overpower your spirit. **". . .Walk in the Spirit, and ye shall not [fulfill] the lust of the flesh" (Gal. 5:16).**

There is a time when the flesh will have to be reprimanded and brought under subjection. Remember the enemy will try to imitate that Lion, but it is not that Lion. Jesus is the Lion of the tribe of Judah. Flesh is like weeds; it needs weeding out periodically. Weeding out is like using weed killer and it includes: fasting, prayer, denials, consecrations, supplications, worship, praise and thanksgiving, reading, memorizing and meditating in God's Word and all spiritual things.

Do these things and then after doing all to stand, **"Stand fast therefore in the liberty wherewith Christ hath made us free,** *and be not entangled again with the yoke of bondage" (Gal. 5:1).* Do not let the flesh (sin) have dominion over you. For Paul said, *"For I know that in me (that is, in my flesh,) dwelleth no good thing: for to will is present with me; but how to perform that which is good I find not" (Rom 7:18).* Therefore; we must " . . .*Have no confidence in the flesh" (Phil. 3:3).* The flesh is unruly so we cannot let it take over and get out of hand. Speak to your mountain, speak to your flesh, and it must obey you. Remember that you speak through the authority of Christ. Also, " . . .*We have an advocate with the Father, Jesus Christ the righteous; And he is the propitiation for our sins: and not for our's only, but also for the sins of the whole world" (1John 2:1, 2).* According to the Word, Jesus Christ will intercede to God for us.

REFLECTION ~
REFLECTION OF MY PAST AND MY PRESENT

My past takes me to my future, because what I have done in the past prepares me. If my past was not a holy one, then my future will not be holy; that is, unless I am redeemed out of it. Yes, I am redeemed out of all of my iniquities and sins. I have a bright future. I have a wonderful outlook and godly expectations. My heart is glad; it is full. My spirit is free, full of the faith of the Word.

My past has helped to make me who I am. All of my mistakes have become profitable, because I see others through the eyes of understanding and compassion because of what I have endured. When Jesus saw my mistakes and what I had done, He came down and became flesh and was able to say: "I really feel sorry for you. I feel compassion for you. I want to help you and love you through your turmoil, fears, and disappointments. I have felt what you feel, and I am going to help you out of all of it."

Jesus gave us a new future. He came

and shared of himself, died for our sins, and rose up and returned to His Father in Victory. We are now free because of His sacrifices. We are free to experience His past and present: His past with His Father prior to coming here and His present status now back with His Father again. I have a new future now regardless of my past. My present being, now, is in Christ Jesus my Lord.

REFLECTION ~
ALL OF MY DAYS ARE GOOD DAYS

My latter days are better than the first. Through my toils, trials, and flaws I found that it is true; the end of a thing is better than the beginning (Eccl. 7:8). I am being renewed like the eagle. I am trading "Beauty for ashes, the oil of joy for mourning, the garment of praise for the spirit of heaviness (Is. 61:3). My latter days are better than my first. My best days will be better than the worst— the pain, the sorrow, and uncertain tomorrow.

I am receiving double for my trouble, for my bread, which was cast upon the waters, is returning. It is not returning void but has great accomplishment and favor.

I have begun a new phase, a phase of Praise, Worship, and Joy. I have begun A Word phase, a believer's haven, Island of Peace, heaven full of joy and singing. I am as strong now as when I was 30, but I feel like 21. My youth has not fled, my place has been enlarged. I can have all of my years or more; that is left up to me.

I have more of God in these latter days than I had at first. In Christ there is truly no end because end is really eternal, infinite, and everlasting.

Oh, what Joy, Peace, and Love. Oh what Power, Anointing, and Strength!

God is the First and the Last; so all of my days are good.

PART VIII:
KEEPING BUSY

(Author Synopsis)

Keeping busy is always a way to pass the time of day or night. It can override troublesome thoughts and regulate feelings of despair and doom. What helps the most, of course, is what you are busy doing. You should be doing what God has for you to do, and no one else can do your job for you. So get in your place or out on your beat, which is everywhere you go. God needs to use your mouth, voice, ears, eyes, hands, and feet.

There are so many souls depending on your faithfulness to God. You have to train yourself to be faithful and true to your calling. It's just like in the armed services where our young men and women are trained. They have to study, listen, and do repetitious exercises, both mental and physical. Everyone has to be focused on just what they are responsible to do and who they have to report to. It is especially important to follow the rules and regulations as well as the orders from one's superiors.

Therefore, keeping busy, doing the right things, and being in obedience, especially to the Word of God, are all important. They say that just one mistake on the field while in combat can cost the lives of many soldiers. Not too long ago we saw the results of this when a wrong turn was made in a service vehicle; some service people paid a very high price for it. They ended up in the hands of the enemy, and some of them were killed.

While on the beat or field for the Lord we have to follow the same concepts as the armed service personnel. Remember, there are others watching you and whatever or however you do something or react; they will do the same, right or wrong. If you are busy, faithful, and obedient for Christ, they will do that too! Remember, there's an old army saying, "It don't rain in the army; it rains on the army." So I say to you, let the water just roll on off of your back, get up, keep busy and, **never give up and never quit!!!**

SOUL LOVER

Be about your Father's business,
Because it is really your own.
We have to be absolutely sure
No one goes on the way wrong.
Now listen to this song.

Don't be lazy;
Don't think it's crazy
To be a Soul-Lover.
Don't be too ashamed
To tell them His name.
Sing it over and over.

Sing it from the mountain.
Cry it from your post.
Turn in, turn in, and
Change your direction.
It's your choice, a free election.

Virginia Jack

You know what it's like to be in love.
You don't give up; you don't give in.
If refused, try it again.
So for souls you want to win,
Tell it to strangers; tell it to friends.

Nothing here amounts to nothing
If your soul at last is lost
And hell's hot slime,
Which laps up crime,
Will be your only frost.

Don't be weary when you do well.
Save that soul from the devil's hell.
Stand up strong and don't you fall.
It will surely be worth it all.
When you're on call,

Say, "I am a Soul-Lover."

CULTIVATED FAITH

Cultivate your God-given faith.
You were born with it you know.
You believed you'd be fed
And just laid in the bed
And cried to Mom to change your stead.

Now in bed you don't have to lay.
Just get on your knees and pray.
Keep the innocent faith you had
As a babe with bottles and diaper-clad.
Leave things up to your heavenly Dad.

Virginia Jack

YOUR WORDS

*Your words have a mission
So be careful what you say.
You will have to give an account
Of every word and every day.*

*Your words they have a purpose,
Send them firm, strong, and clear.
They represent who ever you serve,
Make no mistake they are preserved.*

*Words, they speak from each heart's beat,
A package deal, nice and neat.
Make sure they find fertile ground,
Or they may prematurely turn around.*

*Words will never return void, but
Good or bad, right or wrong,
Curses, blessings, lyrics, or songs,
They will return where they're sent from.*

*Let your words be faithful.
Let all of them be true.
They will travel far and near.
Some ears good news will hear.*

TRAIN YOURSELF

Train your eyes to look unto Him,
Reading His Word, chewing His curd.
Train your thoughts what to think.
Train them to be still; train them to be real.

Train your attitude; it's best not to have one
Unless it's guided by the Holy Son.
Train your feet what to think and where to go.
Train your tongue what to say and what to sow.

Train your hands with busyness and righteousness.
Train them to work and share doing their best.
Train yourself to study; show yourself approved,
No respecter of persons, living the golden rule.

Until you train yourself you can't train nobody else.

Virginia Jack

Remind yourself to love, let it all melt
Into lives entrusted to your presence,
Into hearts sent to you that are unpleasant.

Train yourself to know all of God's Word
So you don't have to go by what you think you heard.
Train yourself to live holy without a spot or wrinkle
So you can show others salvation is simple.

Even a child could easily understand
When told about the suffering of that man
Who came from heaven because He wanted to—
Suffered, died, and rose in lieu of me and certainly you.

Train yourself and all that is thine.
You have no space to waste; it takes a lifetime
But when your peak is reached,
Then others even more you can teach.

Virginia Jack

THE MORNING STAR

The morning star it seems so far,
So all alone and brilliant.
It has a message for us all:
Keep standing tall and don't fall.

You have purpose and you've been sent,
Though you were hindered where you went.
You are placed strategically odd,
To do a work and represent God.

For the moment you are hanging;
Be the light and shine so bright.
Help bring my children from the night.
You provide and guide your radiant light.

THE BLAZE AND THE BALM

YOU'RE THE ONLY ONE

Sing your own song, for it's the only one
With the sound of your voice.
Walk your walk because it's new,
The only walk that carries you.
Talk your talk; make it clear.
You've been blest with it to share.

Pray your prayer; pray it plain.
Write it in God's heart; sign your name.
Send it instantly or overnight.
He will answer timely, right in your sight.
You're not like anyone else.
God can find you and don't need no help.

Do what you do and do it true.
The same way you do,
It will come back to you.
God is waiting
For what only you can give.
No one can do it for you;
No one your life can live.

Virginia Jack

No one can imitate your feelings as well.
No one can go to heaven for you or hell.
You are unique and you're so loved.
Your presence to God is as the doves
The doves cooing are known from all others.
Critique their uniqueness; they sound like lovers.

So sing your song; you're the only one.
Walk your walk, talk your talk.
Pray your prayer, God will meet you there.
Bend your knees where God can see.
He'll cover your prayers,
Take care of your cares
And will always be there.
So do not be amazed,
And do not be afraid,

Because You're The Only One!

THE BLAZE AND THE BALM

SOUL LOVER OUT ON THE BEAT

Soul Lover, don't take cover.
Come on out in the rain.
You've got a beat in the street.
You've got a vow to keep.

Soul Lover, don't you turn,
Too many souls may burn.
If you win some, they'll win tons.
That's why you must run.

Run through the city from state to state.
Tell it from the housetop—don't be late.
Tell it on TV, Satellites, and CD's,
Newsletter, Telephone, Email at Home.

Soul Lover, don't you see?
It depends on you and me.
Don't take no rap; stand in the gap.
Put those souls on Heavens Map!

Virginia Jack

Soul Lover, don't be ashamed.
Do it all in my Jesus' name.
Clap your hands; open your mouth.
Let the words of your Savior out.

Our Lord has a lot to say.
He'll say it through you; He'll say it today.
He'll give you strength on your knees.
Freely He gives, freely receive.

Soul Lover, let us sing.
Let us sing till the heavens ring
Until the sky's opening scene,
Rapturing all of God's holy things.

PART IX:
REMEMBERING GOD

(Author Synopsis)

No matter the pain, sorrow, and hurt, always remember to keep God in your life. I think we can better do that when we can remember the scripture in **Jeremiah 29:11 that says, "For I know the thoughts that I think toward you, saith the Lord, thoughts of peace, and not of evil, to give you an expected end."** God is not the afflicter of evil things, Satan is. It is a good thing to remember the Lord all of your life, but some people come to the Lord in their later years. God being merciful and good, will accept whoever comes to Him at any age. He says in **Matthew 11:28-30, "Come unto me, all ye that labour and are heavy laden, and I will give you rest. Take my yoke upon you, and learn of me; for I am meek and lowly**

in heart: and ye shall find rest unto your souls. For my yoke is easy, and my burden is light." That particular invitation invites absolutely everyone to come to God. **Isaiah 55:7 says, "Let the wicked forsake his way, and the unrighteous man his thoughts: and let him return unto the Lord, and He will have mercy upon Him; and to our God, for He will abundantly pardon."**

It is easy to put yourself down, but to remember the promises of God can be strength in your life in order to stand the test of trials and tribulations. These things come, not because of God but because of sin, the very sin that began with Adam and Eve. That same sin has affected the whole world and everybody in it. For the young, **Ecclesiastes 12:1** instructs the young to remember God while they are young. There is so much young people can do for God with their time, strength, and talent. But when there is great prosperity people quickly forget God, and when trouble comes, then they remember Him. They will then come back to Him like the prodigal son.

I encourage my children to remember God, to love Him, and to obey Him. You may have to keep reminding your children or grandchildren to do this. They will have a good life doing those things. When I was young, coming up, I felt that church was too confining and that we had to go too much. However, I later found out that church never really hurt me. It was not going at all and not giving God any of my time that hurt me when I left home. Being drawn back into the comfort and love of God was the security that I needed to stand and not fall. It takes time to encourage others to stay on the right track, but the outcome is always worth it when they succeed. It even may take some years. I say, hang in there. Like Jeremiah in **Lamentations 3:19** I can say that I remember my afflictions and miseries and my soul is humbled within me, and through them and following the Word of the Lord, according to **Romans 12:2,** I have been transformed by the renewing of my mind. That mind causes me to remember God always and how He delivered me, loved me, comforted me, and has always had so much patience with me. He loves me.

LET GOD BE REAL IN YOUR LIFE

Let God be real in your life, in everything you do.
Let God be real in your life; He will prove to be true.
Give Him a chance to be all you need.
No respecter of person, nation, or creed,
He has eyes, ears, and a heart of compassion.
He has mercy, forgiveness, and love too.
He will fight and be your enemies' assassin.
He will be faithful and just to you.

Let God be real in your life.
He will be what He has promised to be.
He will open your eyes and you will see
His mighty works and His great love,
Heaven opened and God sent it from above.
He is as real as the sea and summer's breeze.
Inhale your victory and fall on your knees.
Proclaim His Glory and righteousness.
With God in your life, you'll past every test.

Virginia Jack

Let God be real in your life.
Surely He has paid the price.
He did the impossible and sent us His Son.
He defied all of our enemies when on the cross He hung.
He hung unashamed, not looking for fame.
Although heartbroken, not a word of it was spoken.
He said, "Father, forgive them in my name."
Yes, for all of our sins He died.
He suffered and had no pride.

Let God be real in your life; He sent His only Christ.
Although many will mimic Him,
No one can replace Him.
No one could have hung so high,
Reaching up past the sky,
But first He went into the depths of hell.
This is the message we have to tell.
He opened the doors of prison; He Is Risen!
So witness it and witness it well!

LOST AND FOUND

*Come and see what you have lost.
Was it red, blue, or green? What was the cost?
Was it material, physical, or monetary?
Was it valuable or secondary?
Can it be easily replaced?
Is it lingering in your mind? Can it be erased?*

*Come and see what you have lost.
Has it collected dross?
Perhaps you will this day find it at the Cross
When you search with all your heart,
Seriously looking in every part.
Prayfully seeking, set your mark.*

Virginia Jack

*If you dig a little deeper
You may find the keeper,
The owner and the reaper.
He will provide your win.
What you need he'll lend.
You can be forgiven again
And be made whole within.*

*I was lost but I've been found.
I have been humbled to the ground.
At the foot of the cross I found my loss.
It was deep within covered up in sin.
My soul however, was well protected.
In God it will no longer be rejected.
My soul is new and resurrected!*

I OWE YOU EVERYTHING

Lord, I owe you everything.
I owe you for watching while I sleep,
For guiding me like a sheep
Through dawns early morning haze,
To drink in the fresh new day,
For nourishing and quenching thirst
And giving bread while providing purse.

For health and strength of all my limbs,
Making me strong with eyes not dim,
With many blessings overtaking me,
For the sacrifices made on that tree,
For washing my past from east to west,
For ransoming me from evil's quest,
For clothing me with salvation's sheet
To be a witness to those I meet.

Virginia Jack

I owe you for all of the love
That you willingly sent from above
To cover me from head to toe,
Inside out, everywhere I go.
A love like this is not a risk.
It glows and shines; my heart is kissed,
Stamped all over, and it can't be missed.
Happiness is now on all of my lists.

I share this love wherever I go.
I send it to everyone I know.
I also share this with all I meet:
Strangers, poor, and those on the street.
They apologized, repented, and some even cried.
How can I not pass it to those outside?
I am truly in awe the way this works.
The more that I give, the return is rebirthed.

THE TURNAROUND

God has seven spirits; let's face it.
Whatever is taken, He can replace it.
He'll dry the tears; He'll lengthen the years,
Drive away all fears, and continue to bless.

Appreciate everything around you.
Remember how God founded you,
Established from ashes piled in a heap.
With breath from God's nostrils you started to reap.

God sent His Son, the Holy One
To turn around through the cross, blood, and ground,
All the sin He found within, which had us bound.
Then Jesus snatched the keys from the thieves.

God replaced death with life.
He then replaced wrong with right.
He took blindness and gave us sight.
He bottled up our tears and lengthened our years
To eternity with Him.

Virginia Jack

I SEE

I was blind but now I see,
There's much more in this for me.
Overtaken by the massive blessings,
Catching up on life's lessons.

Open your eyes; open your hands.
Receive the blessings of the land—
More than you could ever contain,
Spread out just like the rain.

Give your time and your love.
Give yourself and money too.
Scatter the hope that's on your boat—
On many waters let it float.

It will return if you can discern,
In not many days, from waters' waves,
In the faithfulness of the Promiser,
Integrity of the Master Giver.

THE TREE

Trees are used for many things;
To warm my house and comfort bring,
To sled my children down the hill,
A door to shelter, a floor to kneel,
A church with steeple on the top,
A boat pulled up to my back dock,

Pencil and paper and many books,
Table, chairs, and breakfast nook,
Bed and dresser, wagon with wheels,
House and porch and window sills,
Birdhouse, mouse traps, baseball bats,
Flower vase, violin, playpen, and sacks.

However, the most important tree to me
Is the one that helped to make me free.
It held my Savior high and whole.
His blood drained there to heal my soul.

Virginia Jack

*I think that tree, it represents
All of the many sins I sent
To the cross, laid at His feet;
There He proved His love for me.*

*And though that tree, it was accursed,
We yet use trees to soothe our thirst.
Trees provide for numerous things needed,
Blessing our lifetime and things seeded,
Such as our very little ones
Born in sin, lost, and undone.*

*Whenever you use things made of wood,
Remember for what it once stood.
Though it is not the exact tree
That helped to make us free,
It is related, a reminder you see.*

THE WAY I SEE IT

The way I see it may not be the same to you.
The way I write it could mean something entirely different too.
But if you'll open up, let the spirit fill your cup,
You'll get what is meant for you to sup.

The way I see it, we're all going through life's tides.
So let's bind together locked side by side riding high.
We may not see eye to eye, the outward knob,
But one accord is an inside job.

The way I see it, Christ died for all of us to be free;
Therefore, if you can't love,
That certainly won't hinder me.
I have a hold of the knob to the inside job.

Virginia Jack

The way I see it, there's no respecter of persons
In God's book.
If you don't believe that,
You need to take a better look.
Now, stop complaining and finding fault.
Do like Pilate, wash your hands, don't get caught.

In the eye is fleshliness at its best.
Bypass that sty in your eye of worldliness.
Turn the knob, don't hide; open the door wide.
There standing in the inside job is the Son of God.
That's the way I see it.
Receive Him!

IN LOVE

I am in love with Love,
And the waters ran from my head,
Down my face past my feet and legs,
All upon my bed from above.

It's everywhere and if that's not enough,
The oil is now flowing over the same places.
I can hardly stand; it is filling all my vases.
The love of it all overfills my cuffs.

Love is full of God's promises in
The prophetically, highly anointed wind.
Summoned from without and within,
They meet together and kiss again.

Yes, it is time to realize Love:
The promises, the glory and, finally,
The anointing, the power, the fire,
The water, the oil, the joy, continually.

Stay in love with Love.
Its call is eternal life inside,
But all the other blessings and anointing,
They go along for the ride.

Virginia Jack

"THEE"

For being my friend,
Never leaving, always there,
Never complaining about all my needs,
I THANK THEE.

For always believing in me,
Not forsaking me in life's sea,
For holding me up above the weather,
Keeping me sound, putting things back together,
I THANK THEE.

I give thee all my love's story.
I give thee my entire being for thy glory.
I will always be grateful to thee.
Forever I will praise thee.
I THANK THEE!

PART X:
VICTORY

(Author Synopsis)

"I can do all things through Christ which strengtheneth me" (Phil. 4:13). Our victory lies within our faith to believe this verse of scripture. If you believe, then you will not give up because you know that Christ Jesus does play an important part in your victory. Victory is like any battle on the battle field; it has to be won, and it is not always easy. God promised the children of Israel the land of Canaan, but they had to go in and fight for it. Your mind has to be conditioned to not give up and to fight until receiving what has been promised to you.

Life brings along with it many battles over the years, but as David said, **"This poor man cried, and the Lord heard him, and**

saved him out of all his troubles" (Ps. 34:6). Paul quoted God saying, **"...I will never leave thee nor forsake thee" (Heb. 13:5).** We have promises from the books of Genesis to Revelation. You have to want victory and be willing to not let the enemy overpower you. Remember what Jesus told his disciples, **"Behold, I give unto you power to tread on serpents and scorpions, and over [All] the power of the enemy: and nothing shall by any means hurt you" (Luke 10:19).** Those same words are for us right now. We have to begin to put into practice everything that we hear and read from the Word of God as we have been promised. Don't waver but decide to follow what you believe all the way through, no matter how long it takes.

A godly life will give you more confidence that what you believe will come to pass. We often have to repent because of mistakes or shortcomings. We must not hesitate or be ashamed to do so. Ask God to give you strength and deliverance from any and all ungodly things that may be in your life. This will assure you of the victory that has been promised.

I have experienced many victories because I didn't turn around; all through my test and trials I stayed with God. I waited on the Lord, though not always as patient as I should have. There was a minister that often came to preach at our little church when my siblings and I were young. He told us the story of a hen in the hen house sitting on her eggs. He went on to say that the hen house was extremely hot, usually way over 100 degrees since this was in the South. As the hen sat on her eggs, she was so hot until she was sweating. Every now and then she would raise herself up, flutter her wings real good, and sit back down. Most of the hens would tough it out until their baby chicks finally hatched, but one hen he watched in particular did something different one day. She rose up off of her eggs, left the nest, and let out a loud squawk, and went running through the hen house, right out of the door and across the yard.

The minister said whenever a hen did this she usually never went back to her nest again. Going through some of our trials and tribulations can be just like sitting in that hot hen house on eggs. Some very victorious things will come about if we can just hold out and not abort what is in the making. Don't be like the hen that got up off of her nest and ran away. Stick it out and be victorious.

A CONTINUAL FEAST

I feast among hail and storm.
God has turned my calamities into sunshine.
My misery is turned into gain.
Where once was drought has abundant rain.
Never seen before, never heard of,
But a first fruit of God's promises
Has surfaced for me and healed my pain.
My pain, my agony, my helplessness
Has become my strength, my power, my anointing.
My Lord felt this pain and turned it into Glory.
The glory of infirmities is endurance and faith
To the end of the race.

Virginia Jack

*When trouble comes, simultaneously a table
is prepared.
It is full of the praises, worship, and the
goodness of God.
Rejoicing is heard in the midst
Of the loud, fierce thunder, and glory is
spread
Throughout, and from the swift lightening
bed
The Lord is saying, "Fear not. Come and
dine a while.
Move over, and I will take over, my child."*

Virginia Jack

NEW NAME

A good story never ends.
A poem that's true will not bend,
But stands on the premise of faith,
And passersby will hear and wait
To share and help to change their fate.
Don't have to be a later date,
Now is the day to change:
A new start, a new name.
No more Myra, no more Cain,
No more pain, never the same,
Change your fate in Jesus' name

Virginia Jack

CATCH IT!

The wind is blowing; Catch It!
The fire is roaring; Contain It!
The rain is pouring; Soak It!

The sun is burning; Absorb It!
The eagle is flying; Rise with It!
The cloud is floating; Rest in It!

The wind is swirling; Go with It!
The Comforter comes; Carry It!
Love is running; Embrace It!

Catch the Wind;
Contain the Fire;
Soak the rain;
Absorb the sunshine;
Fly with the Eagle;
Rest in the Cloud;
Swirl with the wind;
Carry the Comforter;
And Embrace Love.

STOP WORRYING!

We worry about things we shouldn't.
We tried to fix it and couldn't.
We should have gone to God and we didn't.
We ran over the rim and blamed Him.
Why worry about things you don't control?
You're no better off than a mole in a hole.
You try to dig your way out of a bin,
And you find yourself back in again.

Watch the examples; listen to your teachers.
Count up your cost before getting off your bleachers.
There's more than one way to run to a base,
But there's only one way to win a race.

When you've hoed your last row
And found you yet have a ways to go,

Virginia Jack

Don't sit down to figure out the shortcut
Or throw up your hands and say, "That's enough."

Brace your back and hold up your sword.
Position your breastplate with the Word.
Don't go in your strength; you'll run out.
Depend on the Lord to word your mouth.

Don't quit! It's not over until it's over.
It's not your battle, by now you know.
Move out of yourself; learn to accept,
Our warfare is not carnal; it has angel help.

Remember the battles won before.
Now! You thought, no need to fight anymore.
As long as there's a world full of rebels
You will always have to fight the devil.

Virginia Jack

SPEAK

Everything makes a statement.
Everything sings a song.
Everything stows an opinion,
Whether it is right or wrong.

Everything speaks loud and clear.
Everything takes a stand.
Everything tells a tale.
It clocks with time's sand.

Don't hold your peace
When you ought to speak,
Because in your neglect
There are blessings you have not yet.

CHANGED

Heated in the fire seven times, couldn't run,
Washed, flushed, and then rung,
Dried and hung in the Son, molded, loaded,
Weathered, and wrapped in gold's spun,

Shined and mined from earth's depths,
Down in my soul, turned gold,
Holy Ghost dug, angel rubbed,
Mind scrubbed, dove loved,

Body washed and crossed,
Heaven's gain and sins loss,
Heaven-ready not earth-liable,
Can now preach, teach, and run revivals.

Now help others through their fire.
Lead them faithfully out of mire.
Watch them turn from ashes to gold,
Night to morning, brand new, nothing old,

Virginia Jack

Changed, rescued from earth's depths,
Hammer hammer, chisel, never miss a beat,
It's all good; this is happening like it should.
I'd rather be gold than a piece of wood.

Labor, toil, and then rest,
Shunned, stunned, and then blessed,
Mourn worned but, nevertheless,
Birth completed; it's in the nest.

Anointed, appointed, power-jointed,
Marrow divided, substance provided,
Solid gold, been sin rolled,
Spirit scaffold, soul-forgiven toll.

THE BLAZE AND THE BALM

LITTLE MIJA

I met a little flower; it popped up after a mighty shower,
Very lovely on the outside but somewhat bent within.
Yet it had courage, faith, and grace;
Searching, looking somewhat lonely inside.
It came along for the ride.
It struggled through the startling weather—
Wet, cold, and windtorn.
But then the sun arose and sent its rays
To ease all those other days,
Misunderstood, rejected, but now resurrected,
To go out into the world and share
And to care for those in the mission fair.
Though this story ends; it really just begins.
The best is yet to come.
It has only just begun.

To Kathryn K

Virginia Jack

HADASSAH

Angel that you are,
fallen from a star,
planted here on earth,
by the way of birth,
know that you are royalty,
on land and over seas.

Called for such you are,
minister near and far,
Power, Anointed, Divinely Appointed,
your mantle it has come,
embrace it you are one.

Hold your head up high and flow,
as your virtuous inner glows,
always let that light shine,
to penetrate hearts in perilous times.

To Elizabeth W.

THE BLAZE AND THE BALM

I DANCED

You can't hold me down,
Not even with a frown.
No matter how hard you try,
You can't look me in the eye.

I'm endowed with power,
Sent free for this hour.
Now I have my chance;
I am going to dance.

I danced through the storm.
I danced right through the rain.
I danced in troubled waters.
I danced just the same.

I danced through the land.
I danced on the sand.
I danced through the fields.
I danced as I willed.

I danced in the valleys.
I danced over the hills.

Virginia Jack

I danced all upon the mountains.
I said "This is where I'll build."

Way up high further than the sky,
    In my Master's eye,
    Until I could even fly,
    But I danced on high.

No, you can't hold me down.
I'm not staying on the ground.
I'm where trouble can't romance,
Because I am going to dance.

I have finally made it.
I've been elevated,
For I have put my trust
Far above life's lust.

I am exceedingly glad!
So if you are mad,
Rejoice and shift your glance.
Come with me and dance.

A VICTORIOUS HAPPY CHILD

There Was A Little Girl And They Called Her Ginnie.
Her Hair Was Curly Red And Shined Like A New Penny.
She Liked To Write And She Liked To Draw.
She Liked To Read And She Liked To Walk.
She Liked To Swim And She Liked To Play.
She Loved School And Went Everyday.
She Had A Mind Of Her Own And A Happy Smile.
She Is Blessed Of the Lord
And a Happy, Happy Child.

To Virginia M. (Ginnie)

PART XI:
PRAYER, PRAISE, & WORSHIP

(Author Synopsis)

The tools of prayer, praise, and worship have been used for thousands of years. The Bible says that after the birth of Enos to Seth **"...then began men to call upon the name of the Lord" (Gen. 4:26).** Prayer is communication between God and His people here on earth. We speak to God in prayer, praise, and worship, and He speaks to us through His Word and the Holy Spirit. We can express ourselves to Him and also ask for things needed for ourselves and others. Although when we pray, before we ask for things, we should praise God and thank Him for all of His goodness and for the prayers He has already answered. How would you feel if your children or someone you knew never said thank you for what you gave to them? If they never showed appreciation, after a while you really would not want to give them very much.

God can speak to our hearts through His Word or the Holy Spirit. We are told that we should always pray and not faint, using the little widow woman for an example in (**Luke 18:1**). Paul encourages us to "Pray without ceasing" (**I Thess. 5:17**). He also says that men should pray everywhere (**I Tim. 2:8**). **James 5:14** said, **"Is any sick among you?"** Let him call for the elders to pray anointing him with oil. When Peter was thrown into jail the saints prayed without ceasing for him and God delivered Him, (**Acts the 12th chapter**). Jesus left on record His prayer, showing us just how to pray through His example of The Lord's Prayer (**Matt. 6:9-13**). We do know that through prayer, things will change.

We can even thank God by faith for what He has promised that He will do. Paul and Silas were locked up and chained in prison, yet they sat there and praised and magnified God out loud. They did this before their breakthrough came. While they were praising God, He caused them to be delivered **(Acts 16:25-40).** We have gone through many things, and all of us have had our Red Seas. Hopefully, we went through dancing. We must learn to go right through the middle of our seas, parting them in half, letting our troubles and cares pile up on both sides, not in front of us or surrounding us. The rocks below in the sea are stepping stones put there by God to aid our passage.

Now we know that worship is a more intimate subject and concentrate. When we worship, we do not ask God for anything we just tell Him how much we love Him and how wonderful He is.

Jesus tells us how to worship our Father God, **"But the hour cometh and now is, when the true worshippers shall worship the Father in spirit and in truth: for the Father seeketh such to worship Him" (John 4:23).** Worshipping alone is not enough, we must have clean hearts. If you aren't sure that your heart is pure, then you can repent, tell the Lord you are sorry for your sins, and let Jesus come into your heart. You wouldn't want to put clean clothes on over a dirty body. When you come before the throne of our heavenly King, make sure your heart is clean. **Revelation 14:7 says, "...Worship Him that made heaven, and earth, and the sea, and the fountains of waters."**

SEA BALLET

Let's dance, hand in hand.
Let's dance in step with the band:
Around, around, toe to toe,
Back and forth flow and flow.

Dance on through your Red Sea.
If you don't know how, just watch me.
Troubles restrained, split in half, piled in two heaps.
The ground and my feet they hardly meet.

Let's dance; let's dance; tambourine in hand,

Virginia Jack

To the holy rhythm on holy land.
It's touch and go, only stepping stones below.
Anointed rocks, no other help I know.

Just come on out of long bondage.
Leave behind tormented days.
Come out of soul's slavery.
Leave behind all of those ways.

Let's dance the heavenly dance.
Don't walk; don't run; let's prance.
Angels in heaven all clapping their wings,
We are not our own; we're royalty to a king.

Virginia Jack

MEET ME

Meet me in the morning.
Meet me when I call.
Meet me every single day.
That's not too much at all.
Meet me at the evening wall.
Meet me just like Paul.
Come three times a day
To that what do you say?

Meet me here late tonight
With no one else in sight.
Bring your midnight tells.
My ears are open well.
If that is not enough,
Today, if you feel you must,
We can really wine and dine.
Meet me seven times.
"Your Lord God"

I'LL COME TO YOU

Don't rush me; I'll come to you when I please.
I'll come when warranted; maybe I'll come like a breeze.
I am shy of vessels not yet ready to receive.
I have patience; I'll wait for release.

You can call or beckon or wave your arms.
I'll come when I'm ready, no sounding an alarm.
It may be swift or nice and easy.
It may be full force or scattered daisies,

Scented roses, flowered perfume,
To saturate your being, leaving no room.

Virginia Jack

No doubt about it, it's the real thing:
No effort, no sweating, just feeling.

You can't see it, can't touch it.
You can only rest and receive it.
A small still voice you can hear
Or a rushing mighty wind comes to linger near.

A fire, mighty, settling upon your head
Or waves of water moving instead.
Don't rush me; I'll come when I please—
When least expected, when most needed.

THE BEAUTY OF IT

Lord, I have not seen you face to face,
But the beauty of what you have made
I cannot erase.
I look up to the heavens as far as I can see.
The sun is quietly leaving and
Between the clouds receding.

The herbs and trees reach up to say,
I have had enough today,
But please come back again,
And I will tell you when,
After the darkest part of night,
When no lights are in sight.

Prepare your next grand arrival.
Your breath is our survival.
We will have another revival
When you finally
Peep out of the eastern sky.
Do not pass us by.

Virginia Jack

Set as yet, be our guest.
No, I have not seen you face to face,
But some of your beauty I have
Been allowed to taste.

The greens, the blues, and yellows;
The reds, pinks, and purples;
The orange, browns and gold—
Your eyes hold each color
In their mold.

I cannot see you, but I can feel you.
I feel you when I look at the beauty you've made.
You surround the ground and reach up high to the sky.
Everything I see makes me think of you,
Maybe because you made it,
Maybe because you put the love
In my heart and soul, Oh Ancient of Old.

MY PRAYER TODAY

My prayer today is simple,
Sincere and full of love.
Help me to praise you more
And worship and let it pour

Way up into the heavens,
Out onto every street,
Pouring out of my heart,
Out onto every beat.

Let me praise and worship you
All through this day.
Tomorrow is not a problem,
There will be a new display.

Virginia Jack

My prayer today is true,
For I am in love with you,
And the only way to prove it,
Will be to let you use it.

Bless all of those around.
Let this love of ours surround
The lost, the hurting, the suffering,
And all of them that are bound.

Let me do things your way—
Loving, giving, and doing,
Leading, guiding, and showing.
That is my prayer today.

IRRESISTIBLE

Irresistible, you are Irresistible.
I collapse in your aromatic mist.
Your presence is an overwhelming rare moment,
Saturated in heavenly spiritual bliss.

I am drawn to the Great I AM—
Into the secret place of the Lamb,
Over hills, mountains, and dells,
Drawn up into heaven's hidden veil.
Caressed and held by His embrace,
In awe of the Awesome on the Throne,
And I weep while kissing His feet,
So unworthy in such Presence to be.

Heavy anointing, billowed high tides,
In the Spirit going for a ride,
So full, so fed, well of blisses,
Showered with flowers, made of His kisses.

Don't disturb me; don't call my name.
Precious encounter, let me remain
A little longer in Glory's place.
This experience must never be erased.
Irresistible, swept into seclusion,
Worshiping in a garden hidden:
Diamonds, sapphires, rubies, and pearls,
Fragranced pillows and myrtled clouds swirl.

Irresistible!

Virginia Jack

WAIT!

Wait! Don't hurry; linger here in my presence.
Don't worry; time is mine.
I can lengthen or shorten it; it is my design.
Wait! Don't go! You'll miss the fragrance, bread, and wine.

Spiritual input signals to weak reception.
Open up; be charged with fresh force,
Natural anointing from God's source.
You're redeemed, made clean, one word from His voice.

Rise up, my son, my daughter, for you have done the desired,
All that was in my heart's chambers.
Roll back, stone, now earth: lies, cries, face the fire.
All has been done; Victory is won, over everything required.

It pleased me to give, forgive, and heal.
All that happened was in my will.

The Blaze and the Balm

Now that it is finished, my word is revealed.
It has returned to me, not void, but at my right hand sealed.

There's no hurry, I will teach and show you all things.
The wisdom of my goodness and what knowledge brings,
Surfaced from the throne, overflowing sown
To those I love, all I call my own.

Don't Hurry! Linger a little longer.
Time is mine; I can rewind and erase,
Cast memories, thoughts of the past, and at last,
Renew, strengthen, and gather all thoughts that matter.

Understanding has no limits
When showered from my remnants
Of nuggets prepared and seasoned
Just for you to grasp and reason.

Bask in my glory, while I tell the story
Of how much my love for you reflects
The love I've had for you since we first met,

Virginia Jack

*In the beginning, and the sun sets for you
yet.*

*Linger in my strength, my floral array.
For all is not over, even this day.
I will fill your cup until it spills
Into your meadows and over your hills.*

*If you will linger just a little longer,
You will understand my melancholy plea.
Come up into sky's pavilion where you can
see,
Where there will be no one here but you and
me.*

*Ecstasy untold, not known, fresh, new—
Rain drops of anointed love
Coming from angels below and above.
Relax, know me, my dove.*

*Wait! Stay! Don't go!
There's more; there's more to know.
Let the milk of heaven's wind blow
From north, south, east, and west.
Take your fill.*

The Blaze and the Balm

INSIDE OUT

Lord, clean my house.
Don't let litter lay all about.
Hose me down and wash me new.
Take my heart out; scrub it too.
Shine me up; shape my mold.
Rake my yard; clean my soul.

Inside out Lord clean my house—
Free from everything even a mouse.
Clean my closets and my floors;
Wash my windows and my doors.
Bleach my seats and clean my sheets.

Wash my dishes hot with steam;
Wash my walls; clean the beams.
Wash my curtains; change my lights.
Let everything be nice and bright.
Take all my garbage out of sight.
Clean all my clothes with all your might.

Wash my ears; wash my eyes.
I will not listen to any lies.
Take my heart out; check every socket.

Virginia Jack

Put love back in and you can lock it.
Then your love will always stay,
And I'll have enough to give some away,

Wash my feet so I won't cheat.
Soak my hands; run your scan.
Remove all fumes; turn on the fan.
Take my thoughts and line them up.
If not like you, pour out of the cup.
Lord, if this is not enough,
Light my fire; turn it up!

By the way, don't forget to clean my car.
My basement, too, or I can't go far.
This list seems to get longer and longer.
That's because I have such a hunger.
So Lord, just clean me from head to toe;
Clean me everywhere I go,

INSIDE OUT.

To Sadie W. L.

REFLECTION ~
THE PRESENCE

There is this huge waterfall hanging over my house. The rushing mighty waters from it pour north, west, east, and south. The sound of water spreading out roars in my ears. It sounds like a symphony seasoned with the patience of years. Perfect timing, rising and falling, every instrument blended precise, melodies finest offering to my soul's source of might.

I cannot tell when it first began, but the worthy performance deserves a hand. Yes, the melody floats and graciously takes a bow. It shuns encore, never really tiring, and I don't know how. Perhaps it gains its strength elsewhere to continuously portray such a flawless grace. I know it does for I have found that it comes from God's holy face. Directed by the anointed choir on high, it connects with my soul, and the drums roll on by. It simultaneously beats with my heart's rhythm. It had to come from heaven; it is God-given.

Virginia Jack

It flows all around the ground, entering into my doors and windows, profound. My eyes see, my ears hear, and I can taste. I can feel and I can smell, and there's no haste. The water falls and let it flow, and let it go from room to room, and I will not assume that I deserve this audible performance. To show that I will accept this entree' now, I fold my hands, bend face and knees to the floor, and take a bow.

PART XII:
PRAYER OF FORGIVENESS

Following is a prayer you may pray to be forgiven and delivered from sin, anger, doubt, hate, impatience, self-pity, and such like and for those desiring change in their life and circumstances. This will lead you to become dependant upon God and not on people, places, things, or even yourself.

Heavenly Father, I ask you to forgive me for all of my sins.
I believe that Jesus is the Son of God and that He died for my sins.
He was resurrected from His grave and is now at the right hand of God.
Thank you for loving me, dying for me, and forgiving me. I confess you as my Lord and Savior now. Lord fill me with your Holy Spirit.
Thank You for it.
Amen.
(Continued)

SCRIPTURES:

"If we confess our sins, He is faithful and just to forgive us our sins, and to cleanse us from all unrighteousness" (I John 1:9).

"But what saith it? The Word is nigh thee, even in thy mouth, and in thy heart: that is, the Word of faith, which we preach; That if thou shalt confess with thy mouth the Lord Jesus, and shalt believe in thine heart that God hath raised him from the dead, thou shalt be saved. For with the heart man believeth unto righteousness; and with the mouth confession is made unto salvation. For the scriptures saith, Whosoever believeth on Him shall not be ashamed. For Whosoever shall call upon the name of the Lord shall be saved" (Romans 10:8-11, 13).

The same spirit that raised up Jesus from the dead now dwells in you (**Romans 8:11**).

About the Author

Virginia Jack, one of seventeen children, spent her childhood in Hammond, Indiana. She later graduated from Indiana University with a degree in communications and Calumet College of St. Joseph with a degree in religious studies. Virginia went on to earn a M.S degree in education from Purdue University and is currently completing a doctorate degree in education. She retired after twenty-five years of service with the government. With varied experience in ministry, Virginia is an ordained minister, founder/president of Prayer, Press, & Praise, Ministries Inc., is a sought-after speaker who remains active in her local church (prayer ministry, and cell-group leader), and counsels hurting and abused women. She currently resides in Tulsa, Oklahoma, where she enjoys writing, gardening, and painting. However, when she gets the chance, she spends time going to visit her six grown children and twenty grandchildren—ten boys; ten girls!

Contact Virginia Jack
Post Office Box 702945
Tulsa, Oklahoma 74170-2945
Phone 918.592.0028

or order more copies of this book at

TATE PUBLISHING, LLC

127 East Trade Center Terrace
Mustang, Oklahoma 73064

(888) 361 - 9473

Tate Publishing, LLC

www.tatepublishing.com